HAIRLINE
FRACTURE

"*Hairline Fracture* is an important story by a survivor of a childhood traumatic brain injury. In a voice that is sometime wrenching, sometimes comic, but always fully human, Jodi Gilroy helps us understand the tragic loss, bitter struggles, and gradual change and renewal that survivors endure. Anyone who wants to understand what a family endures when a loved one suffers a brain injury should read this inspiring saga. In its gripping pages, the everyday reality of TBI leaps into stark humanity."

—Joel Goldstein
Executive Director of The Brain Alternative Rehabilitation Therapies Foundation

"In her memoir, *Hairline Fracture,* author Jodi Gilroy offers a window into the life of her eight-year-old self who has suffered from a traumatic brain injury. She then takes us on an emotional journey of her continued struggles in which her pain is palpable. An adult Gilroy then gives us hope for the future by describing her winding path from trauma and grief to self-awareness and healing. A story of perseverance and strength that is a must read. We can all learn from Gilroy's experiences."

—Dr. MaryBeth Crane
Author, *Drop the S: Recovering from Superwoman Syndrome*

"Jodi Gilroy's journey is one of heartbreak, courage, strength, and inspiration. Her raw vulnerability will draw you in and hold you close, then her perseverance will lift you up. The way she has stayed the course to heal and triumph over her devastating circumstances will make you believe you can overcome absolutely anything!"

—Lindsey Jacobs
Author, *Stronger: From Trials to*
Triathlete to Triumphant

"I sat and read this book with tears in my eyes and vivid trauma in my mind, feeling that deep masked sadness and struggle that inspires us. Jodi Gilroy's story is brilliant and her writing exquisite. She has taken the stumbling blocks in life and built bridges instead of walls through her personal journey. Her message is rich and powerful and life changing. YOU ARE A WARRIOR – keep sharing your voice!"

—Kris Tennant, OTR/MPT
Interim President Sparrow Clinton Hospital

"I couldn't stop reading this book. Written with raw honesty of that angry and confused eight-year-old, Jodi Gilroy's story transported me back to 1984, that blue Chevette, the accident, and the overwhelming dread and shame that she carried as a child. If she meant to give voice to TBI and to the challenges it presents for survivors, she did so not as a victim, but as a champion. This book will change lives."

—Tina Sprinkle
Health and Wellness Consultant,
Tina Sprinkle Retreats

HAIRLINE FRACTURE

*Living a Full Life after a
Traumatic Brain Injury*

Jodi Gilroy

Stonebrook Publishing
Saint Louis, Missouri

A STONEBROOK PUBLISHING BOOK

©2022, Jodi Gilroy

This book was guided in development and
edited by Nancy L. Erickson, The Book Professor®

TheBookProfessor.com

Library of Congress Control Number: 2022910873

Paperback ISBN: 978-1-955711-16-6

eBook ISBN: 978-1-955711-17-3

www.stonebrookpublishing.net

PRINTED IN THE UNITED STATES OF AMERICA

DEDICATION

For my sons, Phillip and Neal Addiss. I love you selflessly.
You inspire me to be the best version of myself.

CONTENTS

INTRODUCTION

I t's taken thirty-six years to tell my story and to heal from the trauma caused by a life-altering car accident where I incurred a traumatic brain injury. Rather than viewing myself as a survivor, I felt I was a victim and allowed myself to be victimized repeatedly. I was bullied, harmed, emotionally abused, and worse—I emotionally abused myself.

I believed that my right to live had died after my accident, and then again when my father died. When my son died, I knew that in order to survive and thrive in this life, I had to change myself. To save myself meant saving the little girl and the young woman I'd previously abandoned.

The adult woman within me mothered my inner child, the little girl within who'd been victimized and the young woman who allowed herself to be abused. Then, and only then, did I allow people to see the beautiful woman I'd become, the woman I'd hidden for so long.

This is my journey of emotional and physical healing, a journey meant to inspire you to begin your own. And through it, I encourage you to find your own emotional recovery, so you can live a life filled with inner peace.

My journey took me on many routes. I saw a variety of therapists and received many misdiagnoses. Sometimes I wandered in the wrong direction, but I always found someone who guided me on the right path, and finally, I found the right therapist, the right doctors, and the correct diagnosis.

If you're reading this book and have experienced trauma, grief, or migraines, then I know you've tried numerous treatments as well. If you haven't found the right one, keep going. Your solution is out there. It took me a long time, but with a team of physicians, we've found a treatment plan that works for me. Of course, there's no magic pill, but there is relief.

I learned many lessons along the way, the most important being the value of family, friends, and human connection, understanding that forgiveness does not mean forgetting and that relationships develop and change.

Using trauma-informed therapy practices, I found success and learned how to unbox painful emotions that were the root cause of my trauma, but I discovered there was no finish line for grief. Trauma and grief don't have a finish line. There is no end; it's an emotion you live with. During my childhood, I waited for this emotion to go away. When it didn't, I thought something was wrong with me, and my inner child fractured.

With love and compassion, kindness, and understanding, I began to heal this little girl, reprocess her trauma, and change her victim mentality into a survivor mindset.

I reprogrammed my thoughts. I changed my belief that my father gave life to me a second time. I learned that it was my dad's belief in me, his hope, and his faith that allowed me to live. But it was *my* strength and resilience that allowed me to heal.

This is a story about my journey, my life. My goal is to help you grow through my experiences; good, bad, scary, hopeful, happy, exciting, each one unique. It's a highly emotional journey filled with hope, compassion, forgiveness, strength, compromise, and tenacity. I hope my experiences help you on your path.

PART I

GIRL DISRUPTED

1

AN ORDINARY DAY

"**G**OD, WHY DOES IT RAIN EVERY NIGHT?**"** I asked, hopping onto the swing. Still curious about everything, I often believed that God was the reason for most everything that happened. The wind blew through my hair, my legs pumping furiously as I reached into the sky.

I watched the back door of the garage, waiting for Beth, Aunt Ginny, and Great-Grandma to arrive. Aunt Ginny was my mom's aunt (my great-aunt) and my cousin Beth's grandma. When she was a girl, my mom lived next door to Aunt Ginny and loved visiting her. I enjoyed visiting her home as well, especially when Beth came to visit.

Beth and I were the same age. We were both bright, outgoing, and eager-to-please third graders, and we enjoyed playing pick-up sticks, jacks, croquet, and completing puzzles with Aunt Ginny when we spent weekends at her home. Neither Beth nor I lived in the same little town as Aunt Ginny, so when Beth came to my house, it seemed like a special occasion.

"Jodi!!" Beth charged through the door. I jumped off the swing and ran to meet her with a big hug, both of us jumping and laughing. Running through the house to my bedroom, I couldn't wait to show Beth my new school clothes and tell her about the third/fourth-grade split class I'd start next week. She told me all about her new school and the new girls she'd met over the summer.

The adults sat in the brightly lit yellow kitchen, beverages in front of them, waiting for us to be ready to leave. My mom had packed my overnight bag and carried it out the door for me. I gave her a tight squeeze before climbing in the backseat behind the driver in the little blue Chevette.

My great-grandma got in the passenger seat, and Aunt Ginny put my bag in the hatchback. She told Beth and me to put on our seatbelts. That was different. I never wore a seatbelt in my parents' or friends' cars. In Michigan in 1982, there were no seatbelt laws. Glancing toward Beth, I saw her put on her seatbelt, so I pulled mine over my lap and clicked the fastener. It felt strange there, tight and uncomfortable. But I was agreeable in nature and did as I was told. It was only a thirty-minute drive to Aunt Ginny's house.

"Girls, I need to stop at Sears before we go home," Aunt Ginny commented over her shoulder.

While Aunt Ginny picked up her Sears order, Beth and I chatted excitedly in the car with Great-Grandma about the upcoming school year and our plans for the weekend. We shared stories about our Brownie troops, swim lessons, and our neighbor friends. When she came back, Aunt Ginny drove across the parking lot and parked in front of Baskin-Robbins. Beth and I looked at each other in delight. A bubble gum ice cream cone, a weekend with Beth, Aunt Ginny, and Great-Grandma! I thought nothing could be better as I refastened the seatbelt across my lap. Beth and I continued our conversation, paging through the Sears catalog and eating ice cream as Aunt Ginny drove eastbound on Grand River Avenue from East Lansing, Michigan, toward Williamston.

That was my last memory of that day.

I'VE BEEN TOLD THAT THESE THINGS may not have happened as I remembered them. Doctors say people fill in the blanks with positive memories to protect themselves from the trauma, and that's what happened to me.

I was sitting directly behind Aunt Ginny as we headed east on Grand River Avenue toward her home in Williamston. A drug-impaired driver was traveling west when she lost control of her vehicle, driving off the shoulder on her side of the road. When she overcorrected, she veered her truck onto the eastbound shoulder where Aunt Ginny had driven in an effort to avoid the collision. When the truck struck our small car, it was moving with such force that the car was sheared in half between the driver and passenger sides.

My great-grandmother, Sylvia Oesterle, died at the scene. Before she died, she was able to give the police her name.

My memories of the accident and immediately after remain childlike and fragmented, pieced together like a mosaic. Like the pieces of the bone used to put my skull back together, I pieced together these shards of information, trying to understand what had happened and rebuild my world. I relied on overheard bits and pieces of conversations. I held the hair and clothes that were cut off me by the rescue squad and in the hospital. I attended special celebrations and retirement parties for the emergency medical technicians who'd rescued me. I listened to the stories and built friendships with the people who saved my life—including the emergency room physicians—and I finally gathered the courage to ask questions and talk about the accident.

None of us will know the absolute truth about that day. That's what trauma does. It shocks and stuns. The details are so unimaginable that your brain cannot grasp them. As time goes on, you attempt to make sense of them. It requires truth from people, honesty. This is what I learned through the honesty of others.

2

BROKEN PIECES

I was admitted as a Jane Doe.

Paramedics pulled me from the wreckage and worked tirelessly to resuscitate my listless body. They loaded me in the first ambulance. I had a large, open fracture on the front right side of my skull; brain tissue, glass, and bone protruded. I had multiple cuts and bruises on my face and eyes, and my respiration had decreased.

A team of physicians began emergency surgery. It was 11:59 a.m.

Since nobody from the accident was conscious, the police were still trying to figure out who'd been in the vehicle. They contacted my grandparents to tell them that my great-grandmother hadn't survived. My grandma knew that I'd also been in the vehicle, and she asked about my welfare. At that point, I was still unidentified, the police unable to locate my parents. They asked my grandmother for my parents' contact information but could only tell her that I'd been taken to Sparrow Hospital in Lansing.

My mother got a call from my grandma at 12:35 p.m. She reports being numb and in shock. Here are her notes from that day:

Thurs., Sept. 2
10:30 accident
12:35 call from Mom O.
    Shock, numbness
2:15 still in surgery
7:00 ICU for recovery
8:00 We saw Jodi
did not sleep that night - stayed in lobby

My father would occasionally come home for lunch, which was where he was the day of my accident. Leaving my brother with our neighbor, my parents rushed to the hospital, where I was already in surgery. The doctor removed the pieces of bone fragments, glass, and hair from my skull and brain until he could see healthy brain tissue. The areas were cleaned, and sutures and dressings were applied before I was passed off to the cosmetic surgeon to repair my facial lacerations. Due to the extensive amount of brain trauma and swelling, my skull bones weren't replaced at this time, and I was left with a large sunken area in my head.

The plastic surgeon repaired the compound fracture to my nose, the massive facial lacerations to my face, lips, and cheek. Working on my small face, he used over three hundred sutures and removed multiple pieces of glass. Finally, he stepped out, and the final surgeon stepped into the suite.

The on-site ophthalmologist repaired the cuts to my left lid, cornea, and other eye cuts. While he found no glass in my eye during surgery, he told my parents that the prognosis was serious because I had a left eye injury in conjunction with a central nervous system injury. It was essential that infection be prevented by applying ointment to my eye every four hours. It would be three weeks before he could accurately predict if I would regain my vision. Today, doctors refer to this as a traumatic brain injury.

In desperation, my father retreated to the hospital chapel to pray, taking comfort in the Lord and offering himself up in place of his daughter. He bargained and pleaded, negotiating for my life.

I would later understand the depth of his pain.

My parents became robotic. My mother held constant vigil by my bed, and my father made arrangements for my brother to stay with family friends for the weekend, then return to our neighbor's house Sunday to start his first day of kindergarten the following day.

SATURDAY, SEPTEMBER 4

The ventilator was removed, and I was breathing on my own, supported by oxygen. Doctors and nurses told my parents I was doing great. "Great" was relative to the amount of trauma I had suffered.

I woke to the staff asking me my name and poking at a rock that was lodged in the middle knuckle of my finger. I rubbed it, and the nurses said they would get it out for me. I told them my name was Jodi.

Drifting off to sleep, I later woke and discovered that the rock was gone. My mom said that it was actually glass, and the nurses removed it easily once I pointed it out to them.

"You did a good job, baby," she said. I closed my eyes again. I was so tired.

I woke again when the nurses asked me to blow into a tube. They wanted to see how strong my lungs were. My goal was to light up the pink balloon. I blew with all my might, even if it was only for a fading second. They smiled, overjoyed with my strength. I sunk back into the stiff sheets again, too weak to keep my eyes open anymore. My lungs were weakened from being on the ventilator, and I needed to strengthen them.

Next to me, in between the rails of the hospital bed, was a large, overstuffed bear. Later, I would name him Boo-Boo. He was a friend who would see me through years of surgeries and emotional pain. In the corner of the room, I caught a glimpse of another toy, a child-size stuffed raccoon that was the same size as me.

Flowers and gifts arrived daily, and my parents told me who'd sent each gift. Slowly, doctors and my parents worked to help me regain my speech and memories. They asked me about what I remembered, and I told them I recalled being picked up by Beth and Aunt Ginny. Gently, they started to explain what had happened. I'd been in an automobile accident. A car had hit ours. Beth and Aunt Ginny were okay. They were also in the hospital right down the hall from me.

Great-Grandma was not. She had passed away. They skipped over the intense details of the accident, which I would overhear in bits and pieces later. For now, my job was simply to get better.

BOYS AND GIRLS I'd known throughout my childhood sent cards and cassette tapes they'd made and recorded for me in their homes and at school, which had resumed while I was in a medically induced coma. They told me about the first day of school—the multiplication tables they were learning, the first week's spelling words, and their bonus word: supercalifragilisticexpialidocious.

I read their colorful cards with thoughtful and loving messages. These were the boys and girls I'd known since kindergarten, the children I'd been raised with, my best friends and teammates. I tried to imagine going back to school and resuming life as I had previously known it once I was discharged from the hospital, but my parents said I was going home to recover, and it would be a while before I went back to school. Still confused, tired, and hurt, I longed to see my friends.

A week after the accident, I was released from the hospital. My mother was my constant caretaker. Mom hadn't left my side since arriving at the hospital. She spent nights on the cot next to my bed, continuously watching me to ensure I was breathing. She helped the nurses when they came in to check my vitals and give me medication. My mom would continue this routine at home. She became an extension of my body, my lifeline.

"Jodi," a kind nurse said, "I'm going to wheel you down to your car to meet your dad. We're going to miss your bright smiling face around here."

I handed Boo-Boo to Mom, so I could get out of bed and place one foot in front of the other to climb into the wheelchair. Mom walked alongside the nurse, and they wheeled me down to meet Dad, who'd already pulled up in the car.

Dad got out of the idling car as we arrived, and sobs began to rack my body as the nurse pulled the wheelchair next to the car.

"I . . . I . . . "—the tears hitched in my throat—"I'm scared to get in a car." My eyes darted back to my mom, pleading for help.

"Please," I whimpered, "just take me back to my room. I . . . I . . . I—"

"Shh, Jodi." Mom placed her slender hand and manicured nails on the blanket covering my lap. "It's okay. Dad and I are here. It's just a short ride home."

"No! No, I'm afraid. We'll have another accident. I can't!" I drew further back into the wheelchair.

"Hey, Jo." Dad knelt next to me. "We can sing if you want. Billy Joel, any of our favorites." He tried to draw me into the car, listing our favorite things to do together, but the sight of the car paralyzed me.

"Jodi, shhhhh. It's a quick trip, just ten minutes. Dad's the best driver you know, and he'll keep you safe," my mom urged. My parents were grasping at straws to get me into the car and back home.

My body shook with fear. I was afraid to get into a car, afraid of another accident, afraid to leave the hospital, afraid of the unknown.

"I don't want to be in the backseat! My accident, my accident!" I finally cried. Mom hugged me close.

"You can sit here in the front seat, between Dad and me. We'll put the armrest up, and you can sit in the middle. You'll be able to see everything the whole way home," my mom pleaded with me.

Paralyzed by fear but too exhausted to fight, I finally let my parents coax me into the car. Mom guided me into the middle of the front seat, where she buckled me in place. Dad went back to the driver's seat, and my mom placed her arm around me. Tears slid down my cheeks as Dad put the car in gear and moved forward from the parking lot onto Michigan Avenue. I knew the roads well. In a few turns, we'd be home. My eyes locked on to each car as it drove past. I watched each of the four stoplights to ensure Dad followed its signal. I was hyperaware of the detailed movements of the cars around me.

The radio played softly in the background, but we were quiet during the ride. As we pulled into our neighborhood, Mom tried to reassure me and encouraged me to sit back and try to relax a bit.

"Sit back, honey. It will get easier each time you get in the car," she said.

"I'm never getting in the car again!" I snapped back.

"You have to," sighed Dad. This experience had worn him down. My accident had changed him. He was used to controlling things. He was used to seeing his family healthy and happy. "It will get easier. You're strong, and you'll be able to do it."

I didn't say anything. I knew better. When I was told to do something, I did it. If Dad had confidence that I'd be able to get in a car, and Mom told me it would get easier, that's the way it would be. When frozen by anxiety and fear, I made decisions to please other people. This was the first of many times my parents would talk me off the ledge when I was paralyzed by anxiety.

I was exhausted from the trip. When we got home, I caught a glimpse of myself in the hall mirror but didn't register my changed appearance. Covered with my Holly Hobby comforter, I fell into a deep sleep, where I remained until dinner. When it was time to eat, I walked by the hall mirror again, this time feeling the full force of my injuries. Vomit caught in my throat when I saw that my waist-length brunette hair was shaved to the scalp. I started screaming.

"My hair! My hair!"

I stared at my face in the mirror. Deep, red scars with large welts ran across my face, the sutures still dark black. I was scared of my own appearance.

I didn't want to look at myself. It was a body that didn't even resemble the old me. I was Jodi by name, but I no longer recognized myself physically or emotionally. I was a different child, a different girl.

My parents covered the hall and bathroom mirrors with Garfield, Nancy, the Peanuts, and other comics from our Sunday newspaper.

A week after I arrived home, we celebrated my eighth birthday. What normally would have been a party with neighborhood friends and girls over for the night was different. It was the first time my neighborhood friends saw me. They were kind and gentle. They'd been told I didn't have any hair, wore a helmet, and my face was very red from the cuts. Their smiles were meant to put me at ease, but anxiety—a word I didn't yet have in my vocabulary—crept into my chest. I was quiet and withdrawn for the first time in my life. My parents' reminders of "Careful" and "Remember, don't run" were drastically different from what I was accustomed to.

I opened my gifts with friends by my side, encircled by party balloons of various shapes and colors. I hadn't been forgotten, but I noticed a shift. While my friends were busy running around and playing on my swing set in the backyard, I sat and watched.

IT WOULD BE WEEKS BEFORE I was well enough to return to school. However, my teachers and principal frequently visited our home and brought cards, cassette tapes, flowers, and gifts from my classmates and other teachers.

Our home bustled with activity. New appointments were added to the Girl Scout calendar that hung next to the yellow phone in our kitchen. My mother's smooth, intricate, cursive handwriting detailed which physicians we'd see—on an almost daily basis. Each appointment detailed the time, doctor, and location of the appointment, some of which took place in our home. Gone were the reminders of swim lessons, catechism, Brownies, and carpools.

The right section of my frontal skull missing, I was limited in physical activity, and I couldn't attend school. In fact, I had to wear a white helmet at all times. I worked on my classwork at the kitchen table, completely disconnected from my peers. My friends were learning multiplication tables, more difficult spelling words, and were reading harder chapter books, while I sat at home and tried to catch up with them. I dreamed of returning to school and ached physically and emotionally for my old life.

My parents tried to keep me social, inviting my friends over for quiet playdates, and I ran errands with my mom. One evening, I tagged along with my brother to his haircut appointment. I stood close to my mother, nervous about the looks and attention I now drew.

"Headed to hockey practice, hey son?" one gentleman chirped as he walked past me.

My heart sunk even further. With ponytails, braids, pigtails, and buns, I'd never been mistaken for a boy before. Mom hugged me closer as she saw my shoulders slump. I said nothing, shocked and embarrassed. Had the man looked closely, he couldn't have missed the fresh red welts and cuts on my face. Hot tears stung my eyes, but I refused to let them fall. I told my dad what happened when we got home.

"Jodi, don't worry," he said. "You know who you are. This is making you stronger." I saw the pain in his eyes. His words told me one thing, his body language another.

My feelings invalidated, I retreated to Boo-Boo for comfort. Crying into his soft fur, I begged for understanding and compassion.

My parents struggled to see how painful the transition was, painful for all of us. I lashed out in frustration, and my normally gentle, agreeable nature was replaced by a confused and angry girl who wanted to go back to the way things were.

We fell into a daily routine. Adam left for kindergarten, and I went to doctor appointments and then completed schoolwork at home. Mom worked relentlessly to get us to each appointment, prepared the forms for school and insurance, and was ready for each doctor. Dad would meet us when his schedule allowed, and it often did.

I sat between my parents, thumbing through an old *Highlights* magazine in my cosmetic surgeon's office. I hated meeting with Dr. Gomez, and today was no different. His office smelled like . . . old people. It was an earthy, musty scent. No other children were in the waiting room. There were a few toys at a small table near the door, a doctor's kit, an Etch A Sketch, Jacob's Ladder, and a few other old magazines. This office wasn't really made for me; it was for old people, my parents' age. I fidgeted in my seat, growing more nervous.

I reached up and fingered the stiff elastic chin strap on my helmet. The elastic scratched and often left a red mark on my chin and neck. Glancing briefly at my mom to make sure she wasn't watching, I quietly loosened the strap, and the helmet slipped down a bit over my eyes. Of course, Mom noticed, and she tightened the strap again. I turned back to the magazine.

"Jodi," the nurse called.

We all walked back to the patient room, where I hopped into the examination chair. My goal was to make quick business of this so I could go back home. I was tired of appointments, tired of doctors. I just wanted to go back to normal. I wanted to go back to school.

"How are you feeling, honey?" the nurse asked, having seen me the previous two weeks.

"Okay. Do you think I'm going to have to wait a long time today?" I was tired of appointments, tired of adults making decisions for me, and I wanted to go back to the way life was before any of this had ever happened.

"No, Dr. Gomez is on time today," she assured me as she took my blood pressure.

"Hello!" Dr. Gomez dazzled us with his bright smile as he walked through the door. He was always a positive burst of energy in the room, full of enthusiasm and life. Different from my neurologist, who saw critical patients daily, Dr. Gomez was in the practice of reconstructing people.

I immediately recognized his pungent garlic smell and started to brace myself for his close face-to-face examination. I adored and respected Dr. Gomez, but it seemed like he'd always just eaten one of my grandma's garlicky pasta dishes. Whether we came before or after lunch, the smell was overpowering. I started to take slow, deep breaths.

Dr. Gomez approached for the examination, and I inhaled one last time. As he inspected my facial lesions to see how they were healing, I felt my body begin to relax. He examined the long, large cut on my forehead that ran atop my head from my eyebrow back to my ear. My heart was now beating furiously, and I struggled to hold my breath. Finally, Dr. Gomez turned to my parents to relay his findings, and I let out a huge whoosh of air!

No one noticed. It was like I wasn't even in the room. A sense of relief shot through me. They were still talking, but I'd missed their discussion.

Wait. What did they say? What was going to happen? I felt like the chair had swallowed me whole, like I was invisible to the adults in the room. They were talking about me. I overheard, ". . . ready to go back to school."

The hairs on the back of my neck stood up. Go back to school? With all these scars on my face? Bald? With this helmet? No one had asked me what I thought. Their backs still were turned to me, and tears sprang up in my eyes.

3 RESUMING A ROUTINE

Initially I saw a child therapist who determined that since I didn't have any learning disabilities, I'd fit right back in with my peers. I explained my worries about the lack of hair, the red welts and scars on my face; however, in the 1980s, trauma was a concern for veterans, not a child who'd survived an auto accident. Children were resilient. Only Boo-Boo provided a listening ear when I expressed my pain and worry.

As I transitioned into this new normal, suitcases filled with sadness, frustration, fear, confusion, guilt, anxiety, and shame piled up outside of my emotional processing terminal. I didn't understand these new emotions and didn't know what to do with them. It was overwhelming. I gave them to Boo-Boo, and he kept them safe. It was a means of escape.

As I stepped off the school bus in the cold October gloom, the cold, wet weather bit into my shoes and through my jacket. Friends and classmates stood waiting behind the six-foot-high chain-link fence that stood between our playground and the street. I knew what they'd been told because they mentioned it in their cards and on the cassette tapes that they'd sent home to me. Their looming eyes told me they still had many questions.

I was gripped by fear and trepidation as I approached the large gate, a few neighborhood friends at my side. My helmet fell forward as I looked down, avoiding their staring eyes.

"Jodi, did it hurt?"

"Hey, where is your hair?"

"Did they really take out part of your brain?"

"Why is your face so red?"

"Jodi, how long did you have to stay in the hospital?"

"I'm so glad you're back."

"We missed you."

The questions and comments hit me like bullets. I had to get away. I walked off the blacktop and out to the kick-ball field. My shoes sunk into the grass, water edging into them. Escape impossible, I tried to wait for the bell to ring. *Walk, just walk,* I told myself. A line of children followed behind me. My muscles tensed, and my heart beat faster. I thought that the teachers and their parents had told them everything. I didn't want to answer their questions. I didn't have the answers. I needed to get away. This was too personal. Thoughts rushed through my brain faster than I could process them. I slowed down.

I had to do something to make them go away, but what? What could an eight-year-old girl do? I'd had no control over my body, and now I had no control over what people knew about me.

I turned and yelled, "Get away! Just go away! Leave me alone!"

These were my friends, and they looked at me, shocked. They were just trying to welcome me back to school. I liked them, but I didn't want to answer their questions. It wasn't their business. I'd been hurt, and I felt like I couldn't trust anyone anymore. I was afraid. In therapy, Dr. Seagall told me there was nothing to be afraid of. But my friends were looking at me, and they saw me differently, treated me differently, like I was a freak. Everyone saw me differently.

The more I tried to explain these feelings to my therapist, the more she insisted that my emotions were unhealthy. During play therapy, I'd put children in ambulances and drive them to the hospital, and she would say that the children should do something else.

"Why don't they go to school?" she suggested.

They didn't go to school because that wasn't what happened to me. I went to the hospital; then, when I got out, I couldn't go to school. Why couldn't she see my world?

It had only been five weeks since my accident, and I understood through my play-therapy sessions that I didn't have the right to be disappointed. My role was to resume school and life as if nothing had occurred. I withdrew from others, spent a lot of time alone, and cried often. Boo-Boo was my only confidante.

I STEPPED OFF THE BUS AND RAN through my neighbor's backyard into my own, then tried to open the door in the back of the garage. In my heart, I knew it wouldn't open, but the rain was soaking my clothes and skin, and I wanted to get dry.

That morning Mom reminded me of my therapy appointment with Dr. Seagall. I'd thought about it all day: during math when I was supposed to be practicing division, during spelling when I was supposed to be copying my words, and during reading when it was my turn to read aloud. I hated my appointments with her. It was another time when I felt like I didn't fit in, another time when I was told I shouldn't feel like I did, another time I was told I should be grateful for what I had.

But what did I have? A stark white helmet, a bald head, a face full of red welts, and a reminder of how different I was from my friends. I sat on the sidelines at recess and during gym. I couldn't keep up in school anymore. My parents were unhappy that I was so distracted. I was frustrated, confused, and unable to concentrate. All the adults told me I should be happy, I should be grateful to be alive, and that I shouldn't feel the way I did.

So, I decided to skip my appointment. I saw my mom in the carpool line, but I got on the bus anyway. This wasn't the old Jodi. The old Jodi wouldn't have broken any rules. Adults used to listen to the old Jodi. Now I had to scream to be heard, I had to fight back, and still, no one listened. They didn't hear my story, and they couldn't understand how I felt.

I was right. The door wouldn't open, no matter how hard I pulled. Dad had locked it. I sat on the back patio step and tried to cover myself from the rain, but the water dripped through the holes of my helmet and soaked the stubble that had grown on my shaved head. The chin strap was wet and cold against my skin. My shoes filled with rain as I listened to the thunder and watched the lightning around me. The weather mirrored how I felt inside.

I wished I'd brought a heavier coat. Adam must have gotten into the car with Mom by now, and I could picture him all warm and toasty. Lucky. I wondered if Mom would come home to get me. I hoped that when she got home it would be too late for my appointment. Then I wouldn't have to go until next week.

Dr. Seagall was mean. When I hit the dolls because I was mad, she asked me why. Why did she think I did that? She'd said that this was a safe place, but then she told me I shouldn't do the things I did. That didn't feel safe. She and my parents talked about what a bad student I'd become because I couldn't concentrate. They said I was mean to people, that I was mean to my brother, my friends.

I wasn't mean. Or I didn't try to be. I was tired of talking about my accident, and that was all people wanted to talk about—what happened and what I looked like now, and how I was different. They wanted to know when my next surgery would be, when my hair would grow back, and who my doctors were. Who cared! When I told one person the next asked the same thing. I wanted to play and run. I couldn't because of the stupid helmet! My life was so stupid.

I heard the garage open, and Mom's car pulled in. She opened the back door of the garage.

"Jodi, you had an appointment today. You were supposed to meet me at carpool. What are you doing home?"

"I forgot," I said. "I'm sorry, Mom." I put on my nicest face, but I knew I couldn't be sweet anymore with these ugly scars. It didn't matter how big I smiled; I felt ugly.

"Well, get in here out of the cold. Let's get you some hot chocolate and warm you up. I'll call the office and tell them we'll be there next week," Mom continued. "You have to start remembering these things."

I was glad I'd missed that appointment, but I knew I'd have to face Dr. Seagall again. Next time, I'd sit nicely, put the plastic kids on the bus, and take them to school like she wanted me to. Then I'd go home and tell Boo-Boo how I really felt. I could trust his dark brown eyes and the stitched smile on his face. I resolved to be more like him, to put a smile on my face and bury my feelings so that no one had to know.

APRIL, 1984

As I hopped onto the exam table, the paper crinkled underneath my small hands. The stark white helmet bit into my ears and slightly flopped about. I reached up, set it straight on my head, and played with its chin strap as had become my nervous habit. It was always dirty, and Mom was forever washing it. It had gotten frayed at the ends, and instead of being white, it was now a dingy brown color.

Although I was back in school, I wasn't allowed to play with my friends during gym or at recess. I often sat on the sidelines, making idle chitchat while they played on the swings. I dug in the dirt and picked at the grass while my classmates played kickball, or I picked at the gymnasium floor and removed the tape during PE. My nails, previously clean and neat, were now filled with dirt, and they flitted to my helmet when the now-familiar rock formed in my stomach or chest. I still didn't have the vocabulary to describe my new emotions: anxiety, panic, and shame. I didn't share these new feelings because they felt ugly and bad.

At home, I either tried to focus on my parents' conversations or ignored them. I never knew which one to do. They were always telling me to mind my own business and stay out of adult matters. But some of this adult business was about me.

And now I was in Dr. Posada's, lying on the exam table. My parents always said he was a great surgeon, but he was always running late, which annoyed me. Why did I have to sit in all these doctors' offices? Why did I have to be in the car that smashed that day? Why did I have to look different than everyone else? There was an endless list of questions that I asked God.

"You know, Jodi," my dad said, "Dr. Posada is from Argentina, a country in South America. He has studied all over the world."

I heard Dr. Posada walk in the door. Today we were going to talk about my bone graft—placing a bone in my skull where the bone had been shattered in September.

Unlike Dr. Gomez, Dr. Posada wasn't one to get attached, and he didn't spend much time "kibitzing," as my dad called it.

"The next surgery that Jodi must undergo will protect her brain from potential future damage and correct the noticeable skull defect caused by the accident. This surgical procedure is called a cranioplasty. There are different types of materials we can use to correct the skull defect, such as her own bone, donor bone, or metals. There are risks and benefits associated with all these options, but the gold standard of treatment is to use the patient's own bone."

My dad had questions. "Tell us all of the treatment options, risks, and benefits. We have to know everything before we put Jodi through another surgery," he said.

"With Jodi under general anesthesia, I will graft her sixth or seventh rib, which means that we'll remove muscle and tissue from the surface of the rib to remove the outer surface of the bone. Once the rib is removed, the muscle and skin are closed. Since Jodi is small, the rib will need to be cut again into two pieces to graft into her skull. We'll attach this bone to the intact skull with wire. Finally, we'll close the incision with surgical staples."

At this point, I could not hold back my shock. "You're going to use a stapler on me!?"

The adults turned to stare at me as if noticing I was present for the first time.

"No, no, Jodi, not staples like from the stapler at your home. These are sutures," Dr. Posada explained.

I remained grounded in my response. "Nobody's going to use a stapler on me."

"Jodi, they're stitches, just like your other ones," Mom cooed to me. "They will dissolve."

"Well, not exactly," Dr. Posada chimed in. "She'll have to come to our office to have the staples removed."

"Will it hurt?" I asked.

"No. By the time they come out, your body will be ready for them to come out, so it won't hurt at all," Dr. Posada said.

"Jodi, let's just get the information right now. I think you've gotten ahead of yourself," my dad said.

Dr. Posada continued talking to my parents while I ignored their conversation, imagining the stapler that would be waiting for me in the surgical suite.

"The second and third options include donor bone and metal materials," Dr. Posada continued.

My father interrupted. "I'll donate my rib. Do I need to be a match? What do we need to do?"

Dr. Posada continued, "There are risks associated with both these options, as well as the first, that I want you to be aware of. The risk for all options includes infection, blood clot formation, seizures, and stroke."

The fact that this surgery carried almost as high a risk as my initial trauma registered on my parents' faces and in my own mind. "The additional risk associated with using donor bone is potential site rejection," Dr. Posada continued.

My parents were quiet for some time. I stared at them, hugging Boo-Boo tightly and wondering what they would decide for me.

My dad spoke first. "If this was your child, what would you do?"

Dr. Posada's eyes filled with tears. It was the first time I'd seen my neurologist show any type of emotion.

"I would use her own rib. It may be slightly more painful at first, but the risks associated with the surgery are far less. Jodi is not my child, and I cannot decide for you, however. I understand your desire to protect her by offering your own body, and I would want the same for my own daughter."

My father had connected in a way with Dr. Posada that I could not yet understand. I saw Dr. Posada as my hero; my father saw him as another father who had saved his own child.

"That's what we'll do then."

It was decided. I looked at the floor, at my chart, and thought about that stapler, trying to figure out what size staple remover they would use to get the staples out of my head. I couldn't understand the bizarre medical world I was trying to traverse.

I sat in confusion, hugging Boo-Boo close. I'd be back in the hospital in June with my head shaved again. My hair had just started to grow back, barely covering my scar.

"I can—I can get rid of the helmet after this?!" I stammered.

"You'll have to wear it for a while after the surgery, but after that, you can kiss it goodbye," Dr. Posada said.

My parents knew this surgery meant more healing and progress, but for me, it meant more months of strange looks and feeling alone. I couldn't be mad—I was still alive, right? I probably should feel happy about this. I mean, Great-Grandma wasn't here anymore, and that was horrible. I hopped off the exam table, put Boo-Boo on my side, and grabbed my mom's hand to walk out the door. As positive as I tried to be, I still felt angry and resentful, and I questioned God.

JUNE, 1983

With Boo-Boo at my side, I walked through the Sparrow Hospital doors—again. These hallways were no longer unfamiliar to me; I'd been there numerous times for registration, lab work, and testing.

Today, I'd have my bone graft. Whatever that meant. I didn't really understand the details. I just knew I was going to have a bone in my skull where there had been one before, wasn't one now, and that I could eventually get this stupid helmet off my head. It was always slipping about, the plastic scratching my ears and the front slipping over my eyes. I was supposed to keep the chin strap tighter, but that just left marks on my neck and made me look even more different than my peers. I already stood out in class with my bald head and stupid scars.

I held Boo-Boo like a protective guard. Over the last seven months, the stuffing inside of him had shifted. His head and body were overstuffed, while his neck was little more than a strip of fur that connected them. His head rocked back and forth rhythmically with each step I took, marching in rhythm with my parents. Their lockstep strides gave me comfort, a protective force for what was to come.

I was ushered to a room where I changed into my surgical gown, and the nursing staff took me to the preoperative waiting area. Boo-Boo was tucked under the warm blankets by my side, and the IV was administered while I held my breath.

Shortly thereafter, Dr. Posada, Dr. Gomez, and the surgical team came out to see me. They talked with my parents and then asked if they could draw pictures on me. I thought that was funny! I was not a coloring book, but they'd brought markers to write on my face and across my body.

I'd written on my own hands and legs before, but having someone else write on my face and chest would be different. They placed the wet marker tips on my skin and started drawing. Moments later, they were gone. I closed my eyes, believing it was only a dream.

With a tight hug, I squeezed my parents and was wheeled into the operating room.

"Do you like bubble gum?" a kind, older, gentle man standing by my bedside asked. I was lying on a hard, silver table that was covered with a sheet.

Thoughts of bright pink Bazooka Joe bubble gum filled my mind. In my mind, I peeled the waxy comic wrapper to reveal the soft, pink, gooey piece of gum.

"Yes!" I replied as enthusiastically as I could muster, my stomach now gnawing from hunger. I hadn't had anything to eat since last night's dinner.

"I'm going to put some bubble gum chapstick on your upper lip so you don't smell the anesthesia when we put this mask on your face. Why don't you hold it while I get some things ready?"

Taking the pretty pink tube from his hand, I placed the waxy-smelling tube next to my nose. I inhaled the tutti-fruity sweetness.

The anesthesiologist turned and asked, "Are you ready?"

"Yes," I replied, the wax applied to my upper lip.

I began counting backward. "Ten, nine, eig…"

"LET'S PROP YOU UP ON THE COUCH," Mom said in a hushed tone.

A crisp, white sheet had been placed on the couch under my pillow. Boo-Boo, whose head and chest were wrapped to match mine, sat next to me as I opened *Little House on the Prairie*. My back pushed up against the soft pillow. The surgery was a success, but my rib and chest ached. I now had bone in that former gap in my head, but we had to wait for it to adhere to the rest of my skull. I felt like a mummy, my head and chest wrapped in gauze that had to be changed every four hours.

4 CRACKS IN THE FACADE

After the accident, fitting in didn't come easily. I often felt unsafe, insecure, or unwelcome among my peers. I felt the need to change, shape, or mold myself to be accepted. Yet, the more I changed, and the less different I felt from my peers, the worse I felt. I truly feared being alone. I bent to peer pressure and to criticism at home and from myself. I adjusted to fit in. All of this left me feeling invisible.

Fifth grade brought a new school—Pinecrest Elementary. I'd spent five years at Central Elementary before the school board decided to close our little school. My friends were divided among the other schools in the East Lansing School District. I would be going to a new school filled with children I didn't know. I became hypervigilant about my looks. My hair was beginning to grow back, and I couldn't style it like the other girls' long locks. Even a pixie cut couldn't be framed on my face. I had to do something with my hair before they took school pictures.

"Judy, she has so many cowlicks!" my mom's hairdresser exclaimed, exasperated.

"I know, Lisa, just do the best you can. Try to style it into something cute," Mom suggested.

With new classmates came new questions:

"Hey, what happened to you?"

"Why do you have scars on your face?"

"You have a huge scar on your head!"

I was always trying to justify my survival, and I felt guilty and ashamed. My peers seemed perfect. I was flawed—deeply—so I tried to hide the inconvenient parts of myself.

I struggled academically, socially, and emotionally.

The following year, my classmates and I moved up to middle school for sixth grade, and we were joined by more students from different elementary schools. And I was faced with answering the same questions repeatedly.

SEPTEMBER 1986

At Hannah Middle School, we were taught in teams, where a group of teachers taught sixty kids. That was our team. That meant that I only had to share my story with the sixty kids instead of the 180 children in my grade. The differences between my peers and me became apparent right away: they were caught up in music, friends, homework, and all the social aspects of middle school. I was stuck in an emotional struggle, trying to deal with the trauma of an accident I thought I didn't deserve to survive. I tried to control how people saw me and focused on why I didn't belong and what was wrong with me. I contemplated suicide.

"Dr. Clark is going to talk to us about his career as a physician today," my teacher announced toward the end of our eighth-grade year.

Dr. Clark droned on about his job as the head of the Emergency Room at Sparrow Hospital. I knew Dr. Clark and was very familiar with other doctors and their jobs, so I doodled on the paper in front of me, lifting my head every now and then so I didn't seem too distracted.

"Can you tell us about a patient you thought was going to die? Like, who was the worst patient you've seen?" one of the divas chirped as Dr. Clark drew his presentation to a close.

"A little girl came to the emergency room years ago. The trauma rescue team didn't think she would live." He paused and looked at us. I looked down. I knew who he was talking about. I'd heard my story many times.

"Her skull had been fractured and shattered, and they had to remove the fragments of skull and glass from her head, in her brain." There were now whispers through the room; my face burned. I couldn't lift my head.

"There are times when miracles happen, and the doctors are just there doing the best that they can. That little girl was a miracle."

I felt like all eyes were on me now. I looked up, shocked. Dr. Clark had disclosed intimate details of my story, told them about the tiny bits of brain removed with glass fragments, details I'd hid in shame. When Dr. Clark's eyes met my own, which were now brimming in tears, he was stunned. He hadn't known I was in the room

The bell rang, and we gathered our materials and left the classroom. Numb, I walked down the three flights of stairs and went to the pay phone that hung in the entryway of our school. I took the two dimes I kept in my penny loafers for an emergency like this and dialed my dad's work number.

"Hi, Kathy. Is my dad there?" The secretary put me on hold, and my dad picked up immediately. I normally didn't call during school hours.

"Dad, Dr. Clark was …" My throat closed.

"He already called," Dad said. "He feels horrible, Jodi. It's going to be okay."

"Please, just come get me."

"I'm on my way, Sis," he said, using my nickname—the name he used when he knew he couldn't fix something. "Get your stuff and wait in the office."

I followed his instructions. Like a robot, I walked back up the stairs, emptied my locker, and went to the office to wait for my rescue.

As I walked into school the next day, I tried to steady my nerves and strengthen myself for the questions to come. Dad had driven me, so I could avoid the bus.

When I entered the combination to my locker, my hand touched the hot, tacky, white mucus. I pulled back my hand, tears flooding my eyes. I looked around. Andy and his friends were laughing. I was filled with shame when I realized he'd spit large, gooey mucus on the lock to my locker again.

I raced across the hall to the girls' bathroom to wash the mess off my hand and cry in silence. I felt like I was never going to escape this punishment. I didn't know what I'd done to deserve this. When I came out, the boys were still laughing.

I opened my locker to put my backpack in and realized there was something on the top shelf. Tentatively I pulled it out. It was a gift bag wrapped with a neat bow, filled with dog biscuits. The boys laughed even harder.

"Hey, Grody, like your gift?"

I took the supplies for the first hour out of my locker, threw the rest of my belongings in the locker, grabbed the bag, and went back into the girls' bathroom. I stood there sobbing, holding the bag. I didn't know what to do with these dog biscuits. Throw them away, tell someone? I mean, what could anyone do? How could they help me? This bullying had been going on all year, and no one had cared enough to do anything. I went into a stall and sat down to cry. I sat and sobbed; the hot tears I'd kept locked inside all year finally fell. I knew the boys outside the bathroom could hear me, but I didn't have the strength to care anymore.

Arriving home that evening, I told my parents what had happened. They were disgusted. It wasn't the first time I'd told them about the abuse I endured at school. They'd called the principal before, who told them that punishing the boys would only result in more teasing. This time, my parents decided to meet with the principal.

The intercom buzzed in English class that day, and the secretary called me to the office. My teacher gave me one of her curious glances. She knew little about me outside of class except that I was not a troublemaker. The other students began to whisper in the background, and I tried to tune them out.

When I got to the office, I saw my parents in the principal's office. I made my way in, mid-conversation.

". . . want something done." My dad sounded firm. This was the voice he used when I got in trouble. "This is unacceptable."

"Mr. Gilroy, I don't know what you want me to do. As I've told you before, when it comes to teasing, these boys are going to pick on your daughter even more if we speak with them. I've seen this before."

"Then talk to their parents," he said.

"No, Dad," I interrupted. "I don't want them to pick on me worse. If you think it's going to be worse, then don't do anything. It can't be worse. It's already so bad. I can't stand it anymore," I stammered, tears spilling down my cheeks. I was begging the adults in this room to understand, to help me.

"Jodi, we can watch for them, and if we see them, we can stop it. I'll tell your teachers to watch, but that's all we can do," the principal said.

My mother sat there, defeated and shocked that the school would do nothing to help me.

"We'll take her home with us today," my father announced as he ended the meeting, "Jodi, go get your belongings."

I looked at my mom, who nodded and made quick business of the three flights of stairs. When my father was upset, I didn't argue with him. He'd already seen me hurt and didn't want my pain to continue.

That night, my parents called me into the living room. I knew I was in for a lecture.

"We can't continue to bring you home each time a child picks on you. We're sorry," my father began. "I know how hard this must be. It's April, and the school year is almost over. Mom and I have talked about this, and we agree."

"But Dad, they don't like me, and I don't want to cry in front of them. It's horrible! They're mean. I hate it."

"You can make it through to the end of the school year. You are strong, stronger than you give yourself credit for."

He continued his pep talk while I picked at the couch cushion. I knew what was expected of me. I would do what I was told. I would go to school. I would tolerate the cruel remarks, the spitting, the name-calling.

"Next year, you'll be in high school. High schoolers are more mature. There will be new kids, and it will be easier to fit in," Mom chimed in.

I rolled my eyes. I already knew which kids were hanging out together and what they had already been told about me. *Just great,* I told myself. Another four years of this.

I couldn't control the bullying, and neither could the adults who were supposed to keep me safe. I no longer loved myself. Instead of focusing on myself, I was trying to fit in with my peers. I'd shifted my beliefs to match theirs. Instead of being confident regardless of my looks, I was controlled by the knowledge that my peers didn't accept me because of them. Filled with shame, I just wanted to hear that it was okay for other people not to like me and that I didn't have to fit in with anyone as long as I loved myself.

I struggled through to the end of the year, finding solace in my best friend, who'd joined our school at the beginning of the year. Amy had immediately accepted me, and befriending me was a social death sentence for her. We were friends outside of school, and I tried to fly under the radar for as much of the school year as possible. Amy had moved in with her dad and stepmom. In a house of siblings, two older and two younger, there were always friends over, and I could get lost in the mix. Her sister, Nikki, was a grade older, and she and Amy took me under their wings. In their room, we played loud music, and they taught me about makeup and hairstyles. They were loyal friends when I was in desperate need.

But at school, I was in a constant state of dread and hypervigilance. I was a victim of my surroundings, and I continued to contemplate suicide.

BY THIS POINT, I HAD PIECED together most of the automobile accident through overheard conversations between my parents, their friends, our family, newspaper articles, and a video of a news story that we kept at home. My parents encouraged me to ask questions to satisfy my curiosity. We'd all been through so much, and I blamed myself because I had asked to go with Aunt Ginny.

My mom had kept the clothes and the hair that were cut off me at the scene of the accident. I don't think she knew what to do with them. I often held them as a reminder of what could have been. I fully saw myself as a victim, and I saw the woman who caused the accident as my abuser.

My parents encouraged me to write a letter to her in hopes that it would help me heal. My father said he would find her address, and he would mail the letter. They believed it was essential for me to get my feelings out on paper. Somehow, I worked up the strength to let them do that.

DEAR SHARON,

I DON'T EVEN KNOW IF YOU KNOW MY NAME, BUT IT'S JODI, AND I DON'T WANT YOU TO EVER FORGET IT. YOU CHANGED MY LIFE. I COULD HAVE ACCOMPLISHED SO MUCH IF IT WEREN'T FOR YOU. NOW, I CAN'T FOCUS AT SCHOOL. I DON'T HAVE ANY FRIENDS. MY LIFE HAS CHANGED FOR THE WORSE.

AND MY LIFE WASN'T THE ONLY LIFE YOU AFFECTED. MY GREAT-AUNT, COUSIN, AND GREAT-GRANDMOTHER WERE IN THE CAR YOU HIT. MY GREAT-GRANDMOTHER DIED, AND YOU HURT MY GREAT-AUNT AND COUSIN. YOU BROKE THEIR BONES AND CAUSED THEM EMOTIONAL PROBLEMS, LIKE ME.

I KNOW YOU PROBABLY DON'T EVEN REMEMBER BECAUSE YOU WERE DRUNK AND ON DRUGS THAT DAY. BUT YOUR DECISIONS AFFECTED ME. THEY CHANGED MY LIFE. I WAS ONLY EIGHT, AND I HAVE TO LIVE WITH WHAT YOU DID FOR THE REST OF MY LIFE.

YOU ALSO HURT MY FAMILY. MY BROTHER STARTED TO PULL HIS HAIR OUT AFTER MY ACCIDENT, AND MY PARENTS CONSTANTLY WORRY ABOUT ME AND MY SAFETY.

I HOPE THAT FOR ANOTHER FAMILY YOU DON'T DRINK AND DRIVE. I DON'T CARE IF YOU HURT YOURSELF, BUT YOU HAVE TO THINK ABOUT OTHER PEOPLE AND THE PAIN YOU COULD CAUSE THEM.

FOREVER YOUR ENEMY,
JODI GILROY

I gave my dad the letter to mail one evening after school.

About a month later, I asked my dad a question. "Did I ever get a letter back from Sharon?"

"Yes, but she didn't have anything nice to say to you, so there was no reason for you to read it," he said.

I often wonder if my dad really mailed that letter or if he just told me he did to help me process my painful emotions. I never found the letter she wrote back. This was simply another way that my dad protected me.

5

FRIENDSHIPS

Trying to fit in left me playing several different roles: daughter, friend, sister, student. I compartmentalized and depersonalized for survival. Dissociation was a defense mechanism to deal with overwhelming emotions of feeling unaccepted. I disconnected from my thoughts and behaviors and modeled the behaviors of those around me and those expected from me. I was left feeling dead inside, emotionally numb. With poor coping skills, I tried to control everything.

JUNE–AUGUST 1988

THROUGHOUT THE SUMMER between eighth grade and freshman year, I snuck out with Amy, Nikki, and their friends, in hopes that I'd be accepted into their friend group. I snuck out in the middle of the night, went through the back door, then out the back door of the garage. I returned home before the light of dawn. We'd stay out a few hours, walk around, share our teenage experiences, the shared anticipation we felt about starting high school, and talk about movies and music.

The night I snuck out with Jeff was different. I'd never snuck out with him before, so when he called to say he wanted to meet up with me, I didn't understand why. I'd babysat his sister when they lived in our neighborhood, and he'd come to visit his dad on the weekends. He told me what it was like to live with his mom in a larger city. I thought maybe we'd become friends. It was nice to have a friend outside of school, away from my social pariah status. Since he moved to East Lansing, his family had moved to a larger house in a nicer neighborhood, and he was now a senior.

"I'm excited for you to start high school. You'll be able to see me in the hallway, and I can say hi," he reassured me on the phone.

Maybe we would hang out occasionally. It would be exciting to know someone already in high school, and I knew he had a car. Maybe I could catch a ride to school with him sometimes instead of taking the bus. That would be cool. I hugged Boo-Boo, nervous about trusting someone but anxious to finally gain some popularity among my peers.

"Sure, I'll meet you. Where?"

"Meet me at the Chartwell sign in half an hour." The receiver clicked in my ear.

Heart pounding in my chest, I hugged Boo-Boo close and whispered, "Finally, a friend. I'll see you in a bit. Wish me luck." Giving myself another glance in the mirror, I headed out of the house.

Our bodies cast long shadows as we walked on the sidewalk between the streetlights. I felt exposed and knew that anyone looking out of their window could see me; my heart beat loudly with each footstep. I looked at Jeff to see if he could hear it.

"Let's go back to my house and watch a movie. I left the basement slider open, so we can get in," Jeff casually mentioned.

My heart raced faster. His basement? What? I'd never been into someone's house after sneaking out. It was like taunting their parents, just asking them to wake up and catch us. I remained silent.

"It's a finished basement. My parents' bedroom is on the second floor, so they won't hear us. It's how I got out. I've done this tons of times, easy," he continued as if reading my mind.

"Ugh, sure. But I can't stay long. You know, like for the whole movie. My dad gets up early. I have to make sure I'm home. I don't want to get caught," my mind began racing. Scenes of my parents sitting in the living room filled my mind. My father's face was tight and angry; my mother cried with disappointment.

I knew I was disappointing my parents, but I wanted to fit in with my peers. I couldn't say no; it would be social suicide. I could have friends or sit at home alone. I shoved the concerns out of my mind and kept walking.

My stomach lurched as we walked up his driveway and around the back of his house, my heart sinking further into my chest. How was I going to get home? I needed to convince him to walk me back home. *I shouldn't have left. My parents are going to be so mad. I could get hurt. Or worse. Who knows what could happen to me out here?*

"Come on, but be quiet. I muted the movie before I left so my parents would think I fell asleep," Jeff whispered. I followed him to the couch, where he sat next to me and turned the volume back on.

I tried to focus on the movie, but my brain kept going back to the picture of my parents sitting in the living room. I needed to leave. I needed to get home. What if they were awake? Shit, this was stupid. I was stupid. Jeff put his arm around me.

"It won't hurt. It's just one kiss, Jodi."

I relented and closed my eyes, allowing Jeff to kiss me. I was afraid. I knew that this was wrong. I was here to watch a movie. Here to talk and hang out.

His mouth pushed harder against mine, faster, and I pushed him back off me.

"No," I mumbled, "I'm not that kind of girl."

"What? You've never done it? You're a virgin?"

"Yes. So what? I'm leaving," I spat back, trying to get up. My stomach did its flip-flop thing again. My heart was in my throat.

Jeff put his hand over my mouth. I could see I'd upset him. I was stunned, shocked. I began crying, whimpering. All I wanted was to find a friend in high school. This hadn't gone according to plan.

With his other hand, he pulled down his pants, then tugged down mine. I knew what was coming. I'd seen it in movies. I started to gag and bite. He pushed his hand harder over my mouth. I stopped moving, stopped crying. *I should call out, scream. I could wake up his parents. They would find us. It would stop. This would all stop. But what he had started would already be done. My parents would find out I'd snuck out of the house. They would be so mad.* Bile rose up in my throat. I felt like I was going to throw up. I couldn't yell out. I couldn't upset my parents. I couldn't upset my chance of Jeff talking to me again after this. I just wanted to be liked. *Oh, God, how did I get here?*

When he was finished, he got up and turned off the TV. "Movie's over," he announced. "I guess you can leave."

"Aren't you going to walk me home?" I whimpered. I didn't know what to say or how to react. I just wanted to leave, but I was still afraid to walk home alone. It was dark, the middle of the night.

"Nah, I have football practice in the morning. I'll call you tomorrow."

On my walk home, I tried to stay in the streetlights as much as possible. I was afraid of the dark, afraid of being caught by someone. I shook, my heart in my throat, tears streaming down my face. I refused to make any noise. Maybe, just maybe, he would really call me tomorrow, and somehow, we would really be friends in high school. Maybe I would still have a chance at having friends. *Please, God, please. If you are up there, please hear my prayers. I don't want to do this anymore. I can't live like this. I can't live alone.*

I slowed as I reached my street, panicked that the front porch or kitchen light would be on. It was safe; they were both off. I hadn't been caught. My stomach rested back in the middle of my body. I was safe. Well, sort of. I was home.

Reaching my bedroom, I collapsed on the bed and scooped up Boo-Boo.

"It was horrible," I moaned. I didn't have any more words. I lay there and sobbed to an inanimate object whom I had come to love more than I loved myself, more than I believed anyone loved me.

I contemplated telling my mom in the morning, but I knew she'd tell my dad. The look of disgust on their faces hit me cold, and the anger in my father's eyes registered in my exhausted brain. I knew how they felt about sex before marriage. I had put myself in this situation. It was my fault.

Anyway, they were already so overprotective, had wrapped me in a tight bubble meant to keep me safe from future harm. They understood my pain and wanted to keep me safe from my peers. They didn't understand that there was only so much they could do. I just wanted to be accepted. This was a secret I needed to keep to protect my parents.

I wrapped Boo-Boo tightly in my arms and explained my dilemma, then closed my eyes and allowed the darkness to take over.

AMONG THE NEW FRESHMAN, I was pushed through the tall glass doors into our new high school. Air Jordans and Keds squeaked across the over-polished floors as we crisscrossed the building to find our lockers.

My stomach began to flip-flop as I glanced at the new faces wearing flannel shirts and jeans, overalls and T-shirts, leggings and sweaters, Doc Martens, Converse, Birkenstocks. I inhaled the scent of peppermint gum and overwhelming sticky, fruity hairspray. Blood rushed to my ears, and my head started to throb. Again.

More, more of the same. My parents had told me there would be kids who were more mature, but I hadn't seen them yet. So far, I'd only seen the same kids as last year. And more who looked just like them.

"Hey, what are you doing tonight?" I startled, looking over my shoulder.

"Practice, man. What about you?" I couldn't figure out my place. I thought they were talking to me, but they weren't. No one was.

I kept looking around. I stood there. Everyone was talking to someone. Everyone, that was, except me. I kept looking, searching for a set of eyes that hadn't locked with anyone yet. There was no one.

Finally, I settled in on what seemed like two nice girls having a conversation. I thought if I waited for an opening to present itself, I'd be able to introduce myself.

"No, she got Mr. Jones for a teacher. Who did Jake get?"

"I don't know. He wouldn't tell me on the phone last night, but he was telling me about football practice and his older brother." She paused; her ponytail flipped as she turned to look at me. "Yes, do you want something?"

"Oh, I just want to introduce myself, uh, I'm, uh, I'm Jodi," I stammered, realizing what a stupid idea this was.

"Oh, okay, well, nice to meet you." She turned back to her friend, rolling her eyes. "Anyway . . ."

My face was now on fire. My cheeks stung with embarrassment. How was I supposed to navigate high school? How was I supposed to make friends? I thought this was going to be easier.

"Jodi!" My heart soared. I recognized her voice before I even turned around.

"Amy!" I turned, hugging her.

"Let me see your schedule." She snatched the 5x7 slip of paper out of my hand, comparing it to hers.

"You don't have any classes with me or Nikki or Clay. I figured you wouldn't have any sophomore classes. We have the same lunch, though, and some of our classes are in the same hallway, so we'll see each other then."

We both glanced up at the clock. We knew time before school was limited.

"Yes! This is going to be a great year! I'm so excited!" My heart soared. Finally, I found a group of friends that included me. I'd do anything to make sure I fit in, anything not to be shoved out of the nest.

The shrill bell cut through the chatter of friends reunited. I walked to my first high school class, unsure if I was walking toward a death sentence or the first day of the rest of my life.

THE HAIRS ON THE BACK OF MY NECK stood up when I overheard one of the blonde ponytails tell her popular clique that she was going on a date with Jeff, the quarterback for the football team.

My mind filled with memories of middle school, how when I sat down near this group of girls, they'd get up and move when I came close. I tried to breathe deeply and calm my nerves. Even if these girls had picked on me, none of them deserved what had happened to me. I told myself to think with my heart, not my memory.

As I changed into my gym clothes, I continued to listen to their conversation. I knew if they noticed me listening to them, or even if I was in the next row of lockers, I was taking the risk of a snide comment and the laughter that followed. But still, I knew what Jeff could do. If he could hurt me, and I thought we'd become friends, he might hurt her too.

I glanced over again, looking at her fluffy ponytail. I imagined Jeff's hand entangled in it, imagined his hand over her mouth like it had been over mine. I had to figure out a way to warn her without sounding like a crazed nut.

I couldn't just blurt out what had happened to me, could I? I hadn't told anyone my secret, only Boo-Boo.

"He's going to pick me up, and we're going out to eat," the blonde ponytail went on.

"You know, he likes to talk at the football field after," another ponytail giggled.

This was my chance. "Are you talking about Jeff? I know him." My heart caught in my throat.

"Yes, Jeff, and I'm sure you don't know him."

"Actually, I babysat his sister. I'm at their house a lot," I continued. The ponytails started to giggle.

"That doesn't mean anything. He wouldn't even admit to knowing you." Their laughter grew, and my heart sunk. I'd had my chance, and I'd blown it.

I finished sliding into my shorts and T-shirt. I slid the secret back into my heart.

I was going to be late for PE again. Not that I cared. PE was sixty minutes of sheer horror. Assortments of balls whizzing in front of my face, voices and laughter ricocheting off the brick walls, and game rules that I couldn't make sense of. At least I'd made another new friend, Erin.

The first day of PE my freshman year, I sat timidly in the bleachers and watched cliques of girls chatting with one other, scrunchies wrapped neatly around their high ponytails, while guys bounced basketballs around them. A few of the more athletic girls in our class grabbed basketballs and began shooting hoops with the guys.

There were no familiar faces, and the frequency of panic I now lived with rose in my chest, causing my heart to beat faster and my face to flush. I wanted to vomit. I had to find a friend, someone, anyone who would accept me in this new madhouse that would be my school for the next four years.

When I saw the blonde girl doodling in her notebook at the other end of the bleachers, I pushed aside my fear.

"Hi," I said, walking up to her.

She picked up her head to look at me. My heart raced faster. She didn't know me, but I had to introduce myself. I stood there.

"Oh, I saw you sitting here by yourself. I wasn't sure if you had a friend in class, so I wanted to introduce myself. My name is Jodi."

"Hi. I'm Erin. I don't have any friends in class." She smiled.

My heart soared. I knew that this was my chance. My chance to fit in. My heart and mind raced. I started to share with her the ins and outs of my life.

Like Amy, Erin took me under her wing. She brought me up to speed on all the things I'd missed along the way, filling in the parts of childhood I'd missed: pop culture, music, movies, and a laundry list of teen necessities. She introduced me to her friends and didn't mind when I tagged along with them.

BLOWING CIGARETTE SMOKE OUT THE WINDOW, I parked my car among the Mercedes-Benzes, BMWs, Audis, and Cadillacs of my peers. The beat-up Buick Skyhawk had been a birthday gift from my parents when I turned sixteen. It had taken me months to convince them to buy me a car, to convince them that I, too, deserved some independence. I told my father about the cars my peers were driving—the Mercedes his country club friends had just purchased for their daughter, the BMW that the doctor my dad insured had bought for his son. These were parents of the kids he pressured me to fit in with, the parents of the "popular kids." I tried to convince him that having a car might make me fit in, might make the people he wanted me to be friends with accept me. What he didn't understand was that a square peg would never fit into a round hole, no matter how much force was applied.

Getting out of the car, my friends and I stubbed our cigarettes on the pavement and headed toward the front doors of the school. I'd taken up smoking to fit in with Erin, Amy, and their friends. I jumped at the chance to make any connection with my peers. Some of these friends belonged to the burnout clique, and they smoked pot and skipped school frequently. Others didn't fit into any clique, so they floated between these friends and others.

Which was where I often found myself—smack dab in the middle of nowhere, invisible among my peers but anxious to fit in with anyone who would accept me. I was highly vulnerable to peer pressure, rotated between boy-friends to feel special to someone, and tried to be a part of something—anything—to fill the void inside.

I'd kept my rape a secret throughout high school, but it often replayed in my mind. I thought about it repeatedly, trying to figure out what I could have done differently. My virginity no longer seemed important, something valuable. I'd talk to guys about the overly angry girl I'd become, who was self-critical about every aspect of my life and struggled to maintain healthy relationships. These relationships were often short-lived, and I rotated between boyfriends who I expected to make me their priority. I'd stay with them awhile before I felt pressured to have sex with them, and then I moved on to the next boy.

Most of the time, I surrounded myself with a group of cigarette-smoking teens. I felt at home among kindred spirits. They had suffered their own childhood traumas, were chil-dren of divorce, emotional neglect, and often a combination of both. We struggled to maintain friendships, challenged authority figures, and didn't see ourselves as worthy. We kept our pain a secret, hid it. Some hid it behind drugs and alcohol; I hid it with confusing behaviors and by locking my emotions in conversations with Boo-Boo. I no longer reacted to perceived danger, but I expected it at every turn, and I monitored the moods of my family and friends to gauge how I should behave.

I became emotionless. I lived in a world without happi-ness, joy, eager anticipation, or sadness. Anxiety ruled my world. When I felt something other than that, I turned to Boo-Boo, who stored those emotions for me. I believed that if I shared my emotions, they'd be used against me, used to hurt me. I didn't realize I was creating further trauma for myself. I couldn't see that I'd eventually need these feelings, and when I began to feel them, they'd be overwhelming.

My sophomore year, it was still a struggle to look at my facial scars in the mirror. My mom had taken me for makeup lessons and purchased makeup kits for me; however, nothing available at the time was adequate to cover my scars, which were still large, red welts. Their color had diminished over time, but I was still very self-conscious and still attracted attention and questions from my peers.

After a consultation with my cosmetic surgeon, I underwent a procedure to reduce the redness and puffiness of the scars on my cheek and lip.

"Hey, Sis!" I recognized my dad's voice as he put the ice chips close to my mouth, trying to arouse me from the anesthetic.

"No," I mumbled. I was still tired. I just wanted to sleep.

"If you want to blow this popsicle stand, you have to eat some of these ice chips," he persisted, pushing the spoon to my lips.

"Ugh." I opened my mouth. He was relentless. Along with my mom, my dad accompanied me to each surgery, no matter how small. I knew he needed to get back to work.

I tried my best, but my already-upset stomach rejected the ice, and it came back up before it reached the bottom of my stomach. Dad grabbed a towel and wiped my mouth. Mom gave me a reassuring half-smile, returning to her book. I knew that she had time to wait. Maybe she'd tell my dad it was okay to leave, and she would bring me home. I knew my dad wouldn't leave me, no matter how much she or I insisted.

"Close your eyes, Sis. We can try again in a little bit," he said as I dozed back off.

Waking up, I was finally able to eat the ice chips, and we returned home. It would be almost a week before the new tissue would be healthy enough to cover with makeup. Taking a long weekend allowed me time to recover without having to explain the new scars. I was grateful for the reprieve.

HIGH SCHOOL WAS COMING TO A CLOSE, and pulling into the parking lot, I knew I should feel a sense of excitement about my graduation. I'd accomplished something; I was graduating from high school. With hard work, determination, and a fighting spirit, I was going to graduate with my peers.

Five weeks after my accident, psychological testing determined that I was still proficient in all academic areas but would have to work hard in math to keep up. I continued to be told by doctors, "If you had to suffer from a head injury, it happened at the right time. At eight years old, your brain can rewire the synapses, and you will be just like your peers." My parents reiterated this to me often, and I rejoined my friends in a regular education classroom.

In the 1980s and early '90s, it was generally thought that students with special needs should be placed in the least restrictive environment—a regular classroom with special time for pullout services by a special education teacher. At that time, special education services were provided for the deaf, learning disabled, and blind. I didn't meet the requirements for special education services or classroom modifications, such as extended time for testing, small group instruction, and preferential seating used today. It was through sheer willpower and determination that I'd overcome any learning differences between the other kids and me. The education system, along with the medical system, hadn't progressed enough for teachers to understand that students with traumatic brain injuries processed information differently from their peers.

I gave Amy an enormous squeeze when I met her in the parking lot and realized that I couldn't have made it through high school without her friendship and support. Amy and I hadn't left one another's side since we'd met in eighth grade. We'd even been grounded together the summer of our sophomore year because of something she'd written in her diary.

"Jodi, Mom read about us sneaking out in my diary. She found it under my bed," she whispered into the phone. "I'm grounded for two weeks, if not longer, and she's going to call your parents."

"Oh my God! No, you have to convince her not to! Amy, why did you write about it? What were you thinking?"

"I have to go," she said. "I'll talk to or see you when I can. Love you." She hung up with a click.

Head in my hands, I didn't know what to do. I heard the phone ring, and shortly after, Dad called me upstairs. My parents grounded me for two weeks and threatened to send me to a convent. It felt like the longest two weeks of my life.

Amy and I had attended hundreds of high school and Michigan State sporting events, hung out at the mall together, shopped for dresses for dances, cruised around in her car on Friday nights. I'd come to share the intimate details of my life with my closest friend and didn't know what I was going to do without her after graduation.

Soon surrounded by the rest of our friends, I glanced around anxiously, trying to figure out what was expected of me, measuring the extent of the emotion I should be feeling and showing. For some reason, I couldn't get it right. I was consumed by hollowness. I paraded to the football field to graduate with my friends, friends I'd confided in, given comfort and advice to, and tried to make connections with. When my name was called, I walked across the stage, mirroring the pride I saw in my peers ahead of me.

I guess that was it. High school was over.

6

NEW BEGINNINGS

Extended trauma had cut me off from self-compassion and belief in myself. Instead, I felt shame and embarrassment about who I was from things I did and said. When I left high school, I started to trust myself again. There weren't as many cliques to fit in with, and I felt acknowledged, seen, and heard. When my shield came down, people saw who I was, even on my worst days.

Afraid to leave home, I enrolled at the local community college. Wanting some independence, I rented an apartment near my parents' home and worked part time at my dad's insurance agency. Loving the thought of travel and adventure, I longed to be a flight attendant, so I majored in travel and tourism as a way to make those dreams come true.

My parents struggled with my move. They wrestled with the idea of me becoming an adult and relying on them less. They saw me as a vulnerable little girl, and there were times when I ignored their sensible advice.

Boo-Boo also moved into my new apartment, his dark brown, fuzzy head angled atop my headboard. I kept him within reach for comfort on the most difficult nights when I felt especially vulnerable.

"I thought I'd fit in after high school, but I don't," I confided. "Will I ever fit in, or am I always going to be alone and weird? Why did God do this to me, Boo-Boo?" I stroked my bear's fur, tears streaming down my face.

Dad stopped by every week for a beer run, pretending to replenish the supply of alcohol in my apartment. He brought our household favorite, IBC Root Beer—that was his beer run! I knew he'd never give me permission to drink. It was his way to check on me, to see what was in my refrigerator and if I needed groceries, if I'd cleaned my apartment, and to see how much gas was in my car. We'd sit on the couch and chat about his workday and how school was going. It was a welcome reprieve from the lonesome monotony. Before he left, he'd top off my fuel tank, quickly wash my car, then leave $20 in my pocket for groceries.

When Mom swung by, she noticed my laundry.

"Jodi, just let me take it home with me and throw it in with ours. There's not very much," she'd say.

"Fine, okay." I often surrendered to her requests because I knew that doing things for my brother, father, and me was her way of showing her love.

The next day, I'd come home to find my laundry neatly folded and sitting in my laundry basket outside my apartment door with a bag of groceries on top. It wasn't easy for her to resign from the caregiver role that had been her center since my accident.

Moving into my apartment thrust me into a world where I felt more isolated and lonely than ever. I missed the daily contact with my parents and brother and longed to move home again, to have a roommate or a close friend or boyfriend. My brother was busy with his high school routine, and my parents were trying to get used to their almost-empty nest. It seemed, again, like I'd been erased from the page. I stopped by their house as often as possible for dinner.

"Hello," I called out, walking into my parents' house one evening in the fall.

"Hey, Jo," Dad hollered back from the living room over the TV.

Security and comfort filled my senses, along with the smell of meatloaf and scalloped potatoes that I'd been invited to share for dinner.

"Just in time to set the table," Mom said, placing a handful of plates in my hand.

It was a typical weekday meal and seemed as if nothing had changed since graduation, but I knew something was different because tension hung in the air.

"How's school going?" Dad asked, coming in from the family room to take his place at the head of the table.

"Ugh, it's okay. I have homework tonight and a test on Friday. I brought my books to study," I stuttered. I wanted to sound confident in my response.

I watched as Mom took the hot dishes from the oven, steam rising from the hot pads around her. Dad shared stories about my high school peers who'd traveled with one another over summer vacation, the various countries they'd visited—stories he'd heard at the country club. I lost interest after the first story. Most of their friends' kids were already attending universities or would be in the fall. His constant comparisons to children with different experiences, those who'd had childhoods without trauma, left me anxious and edgy. I was scarred, disfigured, incomplete, and empty.

"You know, most of your class went to the University of Michigan," he said. "Where are you planning to go next fall? You can't delay any longer. Maybe Michigan State?" he continued to pressure.

Some of my classmates were attending more prestigious schools: Princeton, Harvard, Columbia, Yale, Northwestern, and Stanford. Others chose careers in the military and joined the Marines, Army, and Air Force—or they were attending top military academies. During the four years I stood between the walls of my high school, I'd been surrounded by bright, highly accomplished peers. And my light? It had been dimmed by my choice to go to the local community college.

AT SCHOOL, I FELT ABANDONED and longed for connection. I was isolated and alone and looked for new friends in the many faces of my new college surroundings. New students sat in class with one another, joined each other for lunch, studied, and got together on the weekends. I was excluded.

Awkward and uncomfortable in my skin, I was unable to mirror the adult students who surrounded me. I was uncomfortable with the thoughts and feelings that now flooded my mind. I'd worked so hard to block out all these feelings. I'd do anything I could to fill my time in an effort to avoid the overwhelming feelings of loneliness, stress, anger, and emptiness I faced daily.

Eventually I made a few friends, including Sarah, and was invited to a few parties.

"Rich will buy you wine coolers if you want," Sarah offered.

"Are you sure you don't mind?" I questioned, giving Rich a doe-eyed look.

"Of course. Any kind you want. I'll even pay. What do you like?"

My mind raced. I didn't know. I'd never drank anything I'd selected myself. "Umm, something sweet. Like berry, maybe?"

"Okay. I'm leaving now with my buddy, and I'll be back in about ten minutes," he said.

I turned to look for Sarah, but she'd walked away to greet some other friends. I didn't know anyone, and I didn't know what to do. Parties were outside my comfort zone. My instinct told me to sit in the corner and disappear. I moved to the couch, sat down, and watched the people around me. They all seemed to know each other. With each breath, my anxiety rose. I had to get out of here.

"Hey, there you are." Oh, gosh, what was his name?

"Oh, thanks," I said as he handed me the four-pack of wine coolers. "How much do I owe you?"

"Nothing except to be my euchre partner." He smiled.

Relief filled my body. I'd grown up playing euchre with my grandparents, who'd passed this tradition on to their children and grandchildren during holidays. My parents had held euchre parties at our home when we were children. The game was often taken seriously, and I'd become a skilled player, depending on my partner-to-be. It was an immediate connection.

"Of course! I love euchre. I'm not necessarily great at it, though," I stammered.

"It's okay," he continued. "I make a great partner."

Is he flirting with me? I couldn't tell. He was much older.

We sat down to play and dominated the table right away. I caught his name again—Rich. We played team after team for the remainder of the night. I no longer felt like an odd wheel. I was sitting at a table with a partner where I fit. I was someone. Someone who had a similar interest was interested in me. This guy, Rich, had helped me fit into this group of people.

Right away, Rich and I became inseparable. He provided the emotional distraction I needed, and I filled my time socializing with his friends and family. I began to party and drink more.

Rich, who was seven years my senior and had more life experience, charmed me with stories about his time in the Navy and trips around the world. He encouraged me to share my past experiences and gave me a shoulder to cry on. He was flattering, complimentary, and he made me feel important.

Within two months, I found out I was pregnant.

WEDNESDAY, NOVEMBER 24, 1993

"I'LL SEE YOU THIS WEEKEND," Dr. Sinclair said at the end of my appointment. I'd reached the final month of my pregnancy, and I was ready for our sweet son to be born. It wasn't an easy pregnancy, and telling my parents about it had been really hard. Dad was very disappointed. Prior to my announcement, he'd expected that I would transfer to a four-year university, find a nice young man to marry, settle into the perfect house, THEN have children. I'd sent his dream sideways. But again, that was his dream. I was used to living his dream, mirroring his dream and emotions.

"No, absolutely not. I have too much to do," I told the doctor. "We have a huge family Thanksgiving, then Mom and I are going Black Friday shopping. I'm going to the gingerbread display at Michigan State on Saturday, then we're putting up our Christmas tree on Sunday. I can't have a baby this weekend."

I was adamant that I'd give birth according to my schedule, that I would be in control of my body, not this tiny human being who had taken up residence.

"If you don't labor naturally by Monday, we'll need to induce you," he said. "Make an appointment at the front desk for Monday morning, just in case. Tell your dad that I said hi and that everything is going to be okay," he reassured me with a kind smile.

Having Dr. Sinclair as my obstetrician had been a non-negotiable. Dad insured many physicians in our community and had the utmost confidence in this kind-hearted, generous, older gentleman. I knew Dr. Sinclair often discussed my care with him and reassured him that my pregnancy—and my future—would be okay, even if it was different from what Dad had planned.

NOVEMBER 30, 1993

"YOU'RE ALWAYS FULL OF SURPRISES, JODI!" Dr. Sinclair said on Monday morning. "I'll meet you at Sparrow Hospital at 12:30 to induce you. My family is headed to Vail for a Christmas ski vacation in the next few days, and I don't want anyone else to deliver this baby."

Rich squeezed my hand. "Do you want to let your mom know?"

"Of course! And Dad. Well, Mom can probably tell him. That might be better," I said.

We got started with a Pitocin drip around 1:00, and by the middle of the night, the pain was overwhelming. My contractions had started, then tapered off, so they started the drip again and began to monitor the baby's heartbeat. The contractions came closer and closer together, and I labored in my back. My body shook with pain, and finally, the anesthesiologist came in to administer the epidural, inserting the needle into my lower spine. I shuddered, acid rising from my stomach, vomit pushing against my throat. I couldn't take the pain any longer. I cried out in anguish.

"Rich, can you please call Mom? I want her to come to the hospital, so she can see him as soon as he's here," I whimpered, my contractions now closer than ever. I knew Mom was eager to meet her first grandson. I'd sent Dad home earlier after we had a disagreement about *Jeopardy!* I knew it really wasn't the show he was upset about but the situation. It was better that he wasn't here. He could come see me tomorrow.

More faces, more eyes, more hospital staff. I avoided their looks, answered their questions, tried to blend into the sheets. Until Mom walked in. What!?

"What are you doing *in here?*" I said. It came out harsher than I meant it to. I'd expected her to go to the waiting room.

"They just gowned me up and sent me in," she said. "The minute Rich called, I left the house," she responded, half-awake. "Do you want me to leave?"

"No, stay. I'm ready to get this done and sleep. Watch, he's your first," I said, exhaustion and tears filling my eyes.

"It's time to push," Dr. Sinclair instructed. He smiled toward the head of the bed where Mom and Rich now stood beside me.

They grabbed my hands and held on as I pushed. I could no longer feel the contractions and needed their guidance. Exhaustion took over. I just wanted to close my eyes and sleep. The nurses, Mom, and Rich continued coaching: push, push, push, rest, rest, rest, push, push, push.

It wasn't long before our sweet boy announced his arrival.

His kind eyes meeting mine, Dr. Sinclair put his hand out and offered me a Tootsie Pop. "You did good, girl." He grinned. "I'm off to Colorado with the family. I'll be home in a few weeks, and I'll see you at my office. If you need anything, call. They can reach me. I'm proud of you. Your dad will be too."

My heart soared. I'd done it again. My body had faced another fight with pain and anguish, and I'd defeated it. Now I had a beautiful child to call my own. Phillip Edward was here. Perfect, ten tiny fingers, ten tiny toes, and the tiniest of nails on each one.

I offer up a short prayer. "Please, God, allow his life to be perfect. Don't let him experience any of the pain I have. Don't let trauma affect him like it has me. Keep him safe. Allow me to keep him safe. Amen."

I snuggled him into my body for a few minutes before they took him to stamp his small feet onto the birth documents. My son was perfect, and I was completely in love with him.

"I'm going home," my mom said. "I'll be back in the morning. Thank you for letting me be here." She leaned over and hugged me tightly. I was reminded of being a young child again in a hospital bed, protected by her love.

Tentative and still trying to hide his anger about my pregnancy, Dad stepped into the doorway of my hospital room the next evening. Tears filled my eyes.

"I didn't think you'd come," I said.

"Your Mom made me. I had a busy day, so I didn't want to come until after dinner."

Mom behind him, she urged him farther into the room.

"Sit down in the rocking chair, Nelson," my mom commanded. "You're going to hold your grandson."

Dad moved to the rocking chair, and I wrapped Phillip tighter in his blanket.

"I don't know how to hold a baby," Dad mumbled.

"You support his head and hold his body," Mom said, guiding Phillip out of my arms and into her own. She showed him how to support Phillip's neck and head and snuggle his tiny body close to his.

Finally, my father looked down at my son's blue eyes. His eyes filled with tears, and I saw his shoulders relax. The stress of the last nine months drained from his body. This new baby, pure, simple, set his heart on fire.

"Phillip, I'm your papa," he cooed. "I'm too young to be a grandpa," he said, looking up at me.

I smile. "You are, but you and Mom will be a perfect Papa and Nana."

Mom's eyes brimmed with tears. It was as if there was no one else in the world but the four of us. Finally, I'd done something to make my parents proud, something to fill the void.

The following year, Rich and I married. It was a small, intimate wedding of about fifty guests, attended by family, my parents' friends, and a few of our own. Phillip seemed to be the center of our wedding. Dressed in his tuxedo, he crawled beneath my dress and laughed in the dressing room with my bridesmaid and me before the ceremony. I wanted to ensure my son had a father in his home.

"Nelson, come take Phillip for a bit, so they can take Jodi's pictures," Mom called out the door to Dad.

Phillip crawled from beneath my dress. A smile covered his face upon hearing his papa's voice in the hall. His reaction to my dad was one of pure joy. Dad tossed him on his shoulder with a kiss and left the room

I knew that it was nearing Phillip's nap time, and he'd be getting fussy. I needed to hurry these photos along, so I could get him to sleep before the ceremony. It seemed like my duties as a mother were nonstop, but I wouldn't have it any other way!

The hustle and bustle in the room continued as the photographer snapped pictures of Mom, my grandmothers, my bridesmaid, and me. I worried about getting Phillip down for a nap and hoped that my smiles were genuine and that my facial scars had enough makeup coverage. It seems that my auto accident was always in the back of my mind.

I looked at myself one more time before leaving the room. Dad's eyes immediately brimmed with tears. He was speechless, still holding Phillip in his arms.

"Well?" I asked him.

"Beautiful," he said and handed Phillip off to a friend's mother who had offered to rock him to sleep.

"Are you sure this is what you want to do?" Dad asked. "If not, I'll take you out the back door, no questions asked," he said. My dad knew me so well, and he could always read the apprehension I felt but was ashamed to admit.

"Yes, of course. Let's just do this. I love you. Remember, you're always number one. You and Phillip." I reached up to hug him, tears now spilling from both our eyes.

The ceremony and reception were beautiful. My parents hosted our guests at the Michigan State University Union Ballroom late into the evening. Family and friends came from across the state to celebrate with us.

Phillip was taken care of by his favorite teacher from daycare. We'd become close over the previous year, and she offered to keep him overnight, so we could relax. It was a gracious and kind offer. Still, I was anxious to get back to my son the next morning. We'd rarely been apart.

Rich and I honeymooned in the Washington, DC, area, and we visited some friends of his and attended their wedding. Phillip stayed with Nana and Papa, learning to say "apple" on their first annual apple orchard trip. Being away from Phillip was stressful. He was only ten months old, and although my parents loved him like a son, I longed to leave my new husband and return to him.

Distracted at the Lincoln Memorial, Rich caught my attention. "Hey, we'll be home tomorrow. He's okay, you know."

"I know, but I feel like I've missed so much being away from him for a week. I can't stand it. I don't ever want to leave him again." Trying to relay these intense emotions to my husband felt hopeless. There was an intensity that I couldn't communicate—and he couldn't understand.

"Your parents are amazing. They're taking great care of him."

Rich's reassurance didn't make me feel any better. In fact, I felt like he was minimizing my feelings. Trying to get him to understand my anxiety was useless. I thought he was the one who knew me so well, but I was beginning to see a glimpse of something different. The empathy he'd shown before was gone, replaced with this aloof tone. Our son was our responsibility, and he didn't seem to understand.

Arriving back home, I realized that if we were going to provide for our new son, we needed to earn some additional money. It would take both of us to provide for our household, and if we wanted to find a better apartment, I needed to make more money. Rich was in his electrical apprenticeship, so his options were limited. The pressure was on me to find something that paid more.

I pursued a new position in insurance and found a job at BlueCross BlueShield of Michigan, and it was here that I really felt at home. It was a place where I connected with women who were like me, women who were working to provide for their families. Most of the women were married, and it took a dual income to ensure the success of their families. I felt like these women understood my struggles:

my financial struggles, my struggles as a young mother, and finally, the beginning of my struggles with my marriage.

We lived in our small apartment, scrimping and saving until we could purchase a home. Our apartment was close to BlueCross BlueShield, so my commutes were short, which gave me plenty of time to take care of the household chores, get groceries, and do all the laundry. And I still had plenty of time left over to enjoy Phillip's infancy.

Two years after we married, we purchased an old turn-of-the-century home that was built in 1900. It was massive, gorgeous, and riddled with problems. I'd dreamed of living in a whimsical older home with a charming white picket fence. I was dazzled by the claw-foot tub and didn't care about what was behind the walls or that the floor sloped. Rich and I ignored all the red flags and bought the home anyway. It was our first house, and it would be our last together.

We struggled to repair all the problems—from the wiring to the furnace, to the old, sagging floors, to the bathrooms, to the walls that needed paint, and the carpet that needed to be replaced. To make things worse, the home was an hour away from my family, my lifeline.

"Seriously, Rich, how are we going to pay these bills? We can't keep paying things late!" Pregnant again and with mounting bills around us, we sat in the dim dining room with papers scattered all over the table.

"I don't know," he answered. "Just ask your parents for the money. They know you're pregnant again, and you know they won't let anything happen to Phillip."

That was always Rich's go-to solution. Ask my parents. And yet, he loved to buy gadgets we didn't need, the newest tools, and new gizmos for the kitchen, and it seemed like each time I looked, there was a new charge on our credit card. I kept asking my parents for money to keep our heads afloat

By this time, I also cared for Phillip one hundred percent of the time. In the morning, I got him ready for daycare, drove a forty-five-minute commute, dropped Phillip off at daycare, and walked to my desk, where I spent the next eight hours. Most days, I skipped lunch to ensure I fulfilled the mandatory number of overtime hours I was required to work each week. Other weeks, I worked on Saturdays, which meant I drove an additional hour to drop off Phillip at my mom and dad's house.

On weekdays, we repeated the process on our way home. I picked Phillip up from daycare, walked him to the car, and sang children's songs to entertain him in the car. Back home, I made dinner, entertained my now-two-year-old, bathed him, put him in bed, finished the chores such as laundry and dishes, and finally fell in bed, exhausted.

Somewhere between making dinner and playing with Phillip, Rich got home from his work as an electrician. His work was physical and often left him tired.

Being a full-time mom without having a break was exhausting. I'd become resentful and angry because I didn't get any help from my husband, and I knew things had to change.

"Rich, I can't just keep asking my parents for money. We need to sell this hellhole. We're losing money every month. After the baby's born, we have to move. We have to file for bankruptcy."

This was my last-ditch offer. I had contemplated divorce numerous times, but there was no way for me to divorce a man when I was pregnant with his baby. How would I raise two children as a single mom? I knew I wasn't capable. The timing wasn't right, but I welcomed the idea of another child and eagerly anticipated his birth.

"Fine. Whatever," he answered. He picked up his drink and headed to the kitchen to chuck it in the sink. Another dirty dish for me to clean when I was done with the bills.

FEBRUARY 11, 1997

I needed to get out of the car! The pain was searing, and I was trying not to yell because I didn't want to scare Phillip.

Phillip kept asking how John Jacob Jingleheimer Schmidt would escape from my belly.

I calmly reminded him that his new brother's name was going to be Neal and that there was a special zipper mommies have that only a doctor can see.

My mom met us at the hospital to pick up Phillip while I labored. Her plan was to entertain him, create Valentine's Day cards to welcome his new baby brother, and watch his favorite movie, *The Land Before Time,* or one of its many sequels.

I'd been on bed rest since the sixth month due to early labor. I sat in our broken down, one-hundred-year-old home, where renovations had stalled when I became pregnant. We had been doing the work ourselves, but once I was a few months along, the renovations stopped. We moved our bedrooms to the living room since the bedrooms were all torn up, waiting to be refreshed. Just before I left for the hospital, Rich finally finished the two upstairs bedrooms—one for us, one for the boys.

For now, I was about to give birth to my second child, and delightedly so. Dr. Sinclair peaked around the corner.

"Are you ready to do this again? You're having an epidural again this time, right?"

"No," I answered. "I want to have this baby naturally." The contractions were coming closer together, but I knew I could do it.

"Why?" he asked. "They make the epidural for a reason, so you don't have to go through pain. Don't put your body through the stress again," he said, first looking at me and then Rich.

"Jodi, just have the epidural. You've been in enough pain for the last few months," Rich said.

"Okay, I guess you are right. I'm tired of hurting."

I was grateful for the epidural because I labored for what seemed like forever. Bright blue eyes shining, crying aloud for the world to hear, Neal was born in the afternoon.

7 UNWELCOME SIGNS

Shortly after Neal arrived, Rich and I decided that we needed to sell the house. We hired his uncle to drywall and paint the remaining bedrooms that needed sprucing up. We installed carpet upstairs and downstairs, finished the bathroom and closets, put up some drapes, and listed it for sale.

We sold our home and filed for bankruptcy. We'd spent more money renovating the house than it was worth. We were upside down in our loans, our credit cards were maxed out, we'd put off car maintenance due to lack of funds, and I was worried and stressed about money every single day.

It took some time, but in 1998, we moved back to my old stomping grounds. Being back in East Lansing felt good. We moved into a two-bedroom apartment with a plan to save money to buy another house in a community we thought was perfect.

I was excited to be so close to the Michigan State campus. We rode our bikes to the dairy store for ice cream, fed the ducks on the banks of the Red Cedar and in our apartment pond. We did all the things I'd done as a child. It seemed idealistic. Perfect.

Rich and I purchased bicycles for ourselves and a bike trailer for the boys once we settled in East Lansing. After moving, then filing for bankruptcy, we were focused on rebuilding. This was our first big purchase. Every weekend we'd pull them around campus and throughout downtown Lansing. I belted each of the boys into their respective seats. I snuggled Neal in with his blanket, binky, and bottle. Phillip got his blanket and big boy sippy cup. They were responsible for holding the bread if we were going to feed the ducks, or our water bottles. They loved their respective jobs.

Once in a while we'd hear one of the boys yell "binky" or "blankie" while riding, and I knew that the item had been tossed out of their buggy, and we needed to stop to retrieve it. The boys chatted with other cyclists and runners or walkers along the path. They were so social and loved making friends.

My mom and dad's house was about two miles from our apartment, so it was a great place to stop in for a quick break. The boys enjoyed time with Nan and Pop. Sometimes we'd eat dinner and ride home. Other times, the boys slurped on popsicles and got a quick hug. We'd often refill our water bottles and hit the road.

One hot Sunday in June, I decided that we'd bike the Lansing River Trail. This had been on my bucket list since the previous summer, and I was adamant we try. Rich was agreeable, and we set off.

It was a cool enough start, so we rode in shorts and T-shirts. I threw some light blankets in for the boys. They liked to slide them under their legs against the hard plastic when it got chilly. They had zip-up sweatshirts on over their shirts to keep them warm on the shaded portions of the trail.

The first half of the ride went smoothly. We'd packed a cooler for lunch, and we grabbed our sandwiches and ate next to the river. The river was quiet, but you could hear the cars on the other side of the trail.

I listened to the boys chitchat about the ducks and nature, and we said hello to each passerby. My heart swelled with pride. My children were kind and loving to each stranger they met.

My head was feeling heavy, but I wouldn't let it deter me from enjoying this day. I'd often felt this way since childhood. I had headaches and backaches, but I always ignored them. I thought headaches were old-people problems. It was probably nothing.

Rich said again, "Are you ready to go? Earth to Jodi."

"Oh, yeah," I replied as I walked over to my bike. My head felt worse, heavy like lead. My limbs were slow to respond.

As we rode, I begged to stop off at Mom and Dad's house for a break. Just a short one.

"Your parents aren't even home," Rich said.

"I know. But something isn't right. I need to stop."

We got to my parents' house, and I let myself in with the key—the same key I'd used since childhood. I raced to the kitchen to drink water from the faucet. I couldn't get enough. I was so thirsty. I was so hot.

"Hey, slow down there," Rich said. "You're going to make yourself sick."

Reluctantly, I stopped. I couldn't get cool, so I lifted my shirt and lay on the air register underneath the kitchen table. In my mind, I could see my body lying there, but I was hovering over it. I was suspended in midair, watching myself. I couldn't say anything. I couldn't move. What was wrong with me? My head was pounding. I wanted to cry out.

I don't know how long I lay there. When I finally came out of my daze, I told Rich we needed to call our family physician. Something wasn't right. My head hurt so badly. I wanted to close my eyes and escape the sound, the light, everything around me.

I listened as Rich made the call and waited for our doctor to call us back. Rich explained my symptoms and made an appointment for the next day. I'd need to take the day off from work.

How were we going to get home? I couldn't get back on that bike. I called my parents, who were up north at their cottage, and explained the situation.

"What do you want me to do?" Mom asked.

"I don't know. I just need someone to talk to. I mean, your car is in the garage. Where are your keys?"

"They're here in my purse. And you don't have the kids' car seats anyway," she replied.

She was right. I had to finish what I had started. I had to ride that bike home.

"Okay, so we're going to ride home. It's going to take me a long time," I sighed.

"It's okay, Jodi. Call me when you get there. I love you," she encouraged.

"Okay, bye." I hung up the phone, defeated.

One leg over the other, I heaved myself onto my bike. It took us hours to get home. The kids were hungry; we ordered a pizza, and I headed to bed, anxious and afraid of what tomorrow might bring.

The next morning, my mind and heart raced as I paced the apartment. Rich had taken the boys to daycare an hour before, and I knew he'd be back soon. But why did my head still hurt? Why couldn't I sit still? Why, after all this time? Why me? Why the fuck me? I had two children now!

Rich's footsteps rushed louder outside of our apartment door. "Come on, grab your purse," he said.

"Already have it. I've been waiting."

"I went as quick as I could. Damn, Jodi," he snapped at me. He turned and left me to lock the door and catch up with him.

My reply had been quick and tense. I realized that I'd upset him.

"Rich, I'm sorry. I'm worried. I'm scared. I hurt right now. My mom's going to meet us there." Stumbling over my words, I tried to apologize, tried to set things right. Our relationship was either hot or cold, at complete unrest, and I felt pressured to apologize anytime he got upset.

I locked the door with trembling hands and rushed to meet him on the steps.

"Please forgive me. I, I, I didn't mean to upset you. Rich, please, I'm sorry . . . please, just listen. Don't walk so fast. Please." I wanted him to acknowledge my fear.

"Whatever. It's fine." He got in the driver's seat, and I swallowed the lump that had grown in my throat.

The drive was quiet, tense. Mom greeted both of us with a hug in the parking lot.

"Rich, I'm so glad you were with her yesterday." Mom was trying to be generous. I knew she could feel the tension between us in the air.

They quickly checked me in and ushered us to the patient room. Again, I felt my nerves spike because there was usually a wait to get back to the exam room.

"Jodi, tell me about yesterday," my doctor said. This was unlike his normal, lively greeting. My heart raced as I recalled other physicians with a similar bedside manner.

"All of a sudden, I was overwhelmingly hot. Then we stopped at my parents' house. I couldn't get enough water, and I couldn't get cool. I was lying on their kitchen registers, but even that didn't cool me down. My heart was pounding, and I could feel the blood rushing through my veins and in my ears. Then I felt myself floating over my body. I could hear Rich talk to me, but I couldn't respond. I wanted to, but I couldn't find the right words to say, put them together, make a sentence, or open my mouth to get them out. What's going on? Do you think this is because of my accident? Will this happen again?"

"Okay, wait. You were riding your bike before this? Yes, that's in my notes. Do you normally ride your bike? How far did you go? Did you go farther than usual?" He tried to gather more details, slow me down.

"Yes, we try to ride our bikes every weekend. We did go a little farther this weekend, but I'm in great shape, so it's not a big deal. I didn't feel unwell. Rich, how far do you think we went?"

"We probably rode between six and seven miles." He looked over at Mom, reassuring her that he'd calmed down.

"Well, it sounds like you had a petit mal seizure. I want to refer you to a neurologist, and I am going to order an MRI and EEG. The EEG will check your brain-wave pattern, and the MRI will check for stroke or tumors. Do you have any questions? How about you, Mom?"

"No, I've had an MRI and EEG before, so I know what to expect." I looked at Mom, who looked a bit dazed.

"Do you think this is related to her old head injury?" Mom ventured.

"It could be. It's more than likely, but I don't want to speculate," he answered. "That's why I want Jodi to see a neurologist."

GUILT AND SHAME BECAME OVERWHELMING as my health deteriorated. I slept more as headaches overtook my life. I took a medical leave from work. Phillip and Neal often snuggled with me in bed or brought their toys into my room while Rich worked into the early evening. I waited weeks for an appointment with a neurologist.

The boys, excited to see smiling, happy faces, would wave and yell hellos out of our apartment window at our young neighbors. The vibrant college students in our building adored the boys, often racing them up and down the hallways and stairwells. I longed to leave this building of individual households and venture into suburbia, where we could have our own home with a swing set in the backyard.

Rich had promised that we'd set our lives on the right track, but right now, it felt hopeless.

I stretched my body, and my joints ached, but I needed to get out of bed and get dinner ready for the boys. It was difficult to adjust to my new medications to control the seizures and migraines. Legs wobbly, hands trembling, I walked down the hallway toward the kitchen, my mind still in a fog. I heard the boys playing in their bedroom, Hot Wheels flying across the tracks, and shrieks of laughter. I imagined their cars taking the curves at top speed. Just like we were trying to take life.

We'd been working through a litany of prescriptions. Some worked; others didn't. Finding the right fit was difficult. It meant weaning on and off medications like an infant on baby food. Nausea, depression, anxiety, and irritability became part of every day. I'd shut the door on these enemies when my children were born. Opening the door to them again was not welcome.

Hearing me, the boys rushed out of the room. "Mom!" Shrieks of giggles came along with smiles, stuffed animals, blankets, and every other toy they could drag into the living room.

I loved my boys, but my heart sank. I didn't have the energy to pick up their stuff, keep my house neat and tidy, and myself healthy.

"Oh, boys, please make sure to pick up your toys if you bring them out here."

I saw their shoulders slump. Excited to see me, that was not the welcome they'd hoped for. They ran to my legs, arms wide for hugs. Kneeling, I embraced each of them. Together, then independently. I listened as they told me stories of their stuffed animals, read me their books, and brought out numerous puzzles to piece together. Planting a kiss atop each of their heads, I made my way into the kitchen. We had to eat.

8 DREAMS FULFILLED

Phillip had entered kindergarten, and Neal was in preschool when I returned to work. I'd been home with the boys for three years.

In 2000, I'd left my job with BlueCross BlueShield because I couldn't stand the pressure and stress any longer. I felt micromanaged, was treated like a child, and missed my children terribly. Their childhood was flying by without me, and we were paying as much in daycare as I earned each month. So, I quit. It was the first of many jobs I would walk away from.

But now I was ready to get back on my feet again, and my dad gave me that opportunity. His insurance office had blossomed since I was a little girl; he credited that growth with my accident. He'd made a deal with God that if He spared my life, Dad would do everything possible to provide for me. He worked tirelessly and endlessly, and in return, God gave him success in business.

Dad told himself that through his prayers, he saved my life. My mother agreed with him. It was as if my mother had given birth to me the first time, and my father gave birth to me a second time. Somewhere, the power of my survival had been assumed by my parents. What they didn't understand was that I'd come to rely on them for my survival. Even as an adult, I never developed the necessary tools or the coping mechanisms required to survive, much less thrive, on my own.

And here was yet another example: my dad rescued me and gave me a job working for one of his commercial insurance agents as a customer service representative. Then when I'd earned enough experience, I'd move on to another position in a larger company.

This did not bode well with Dad's other employees. They were often resentful and would lash out. I couldn't understand this. I didn't understand why they would resent me. In my mind, my life was an obstacle course, and I struggled with new ways to maneuver. Filled with new challenges and relationships to transverse, I was eager to please anyone who came into my life. The shining lights in my life were my sons and the close friends I'd gained when my boys started school.

One day, I struck up a conversation with the mom of a boy in Phillip's class. She also had a younger son Neal's age. I asked if she wanted to bring the boys over for a playdate, and it was the best invitation I had ever extended. Marianne became one of my best friends. I followed her lead and learned to navigate girl nights, Boy Scouts, and other school social activities. Marianne, Nonnie, Kim, Maureen, and Cathy became some of my best girlfriends.

But I was still restless. I loved insurance. I loved the business world. I loved working with my dad. But I could never work *with* my dad. He assigned me to work with other employees, employees who didn't want to work with me and often talked about me behind my back.

I shared new ideas, invigorated to help further the agency and contribute to something that was such an important part of our family. However, my ideas were disregarded, ignored. My father had told me he wanted me to be a part of his business, but his actions were contrary to what he'd said. I felt neglected, shoved from the nest.

Frustrated, I decided that I needed to develop a career for myself. I needed to do something with the knowledge God had given me as a child. I thought He'd allowed me to experience a traumatic series of events to strengthen my character, so I could teach other children compassion and love. I would become a teacher!

That day, I enrolled in classes at our local community college. I looked up the necessary requirements to transfer as an elementary education major from community college to Michigan State University, and with the same impulsivity I'd shown for so many other things in life, I enrolled in my first class.

I popped down to my dad's office to share the great news. He was ecstatic. I was returning to college to pursue my dream. My passion. He knew how much I loved children and thought it would be a wonderful fit for me.

I called my mom, who was equally as optimistic. She knew I would be a perfect fit for college.

"Don't worry about the cost," she said. "Dad and I will take care of the bills."

When I returned home and sprung the news on my husband, his response stopped me dead in my tracks.

"You did what?" he questioned.

Oh my God, he doesn't think I can do this. He doesn't think I'm smart enough. What had I been thinking?

"I registered for part-time classes at LCC," I said again. "I'm going back to school to be a teacher."

The smile grew across my face in hopes his excitement would mirror my own, but it didn't. I saw confusion, tension, and frustration on his face. My mind began to race, and then the fear of disappointing someone I loved created panic. Didn't he think I was capable? I turned on him and lashed out. I peppered him with the very questions I asked of myself.

"Don't you think I can do this? Don't you think I'm smart enough?? What, Rich? What?" I spat at him.

"No," he responded, "that's not it. You just went out and did it. You didn't even talk to me. No one knew you were even interested in teaching, and you bolted ahead and registered for classes.

"You'll have to work part-time now. That's going to affect our income, Jodi."

He was right. What had I been thinking? I was stupid. I couldn't do this. I certainly wasn't smart enough. In high school, I was only average. Below average when I compared myself to my peers who went on to schools like Yale, Harvard, Columbia, MIT, and Cornell. And they'd already graduated. Outgrown me. They were doctors, lawyers, and politicians. Who was I to think I could take on motherhood and college?

No. I wasn't good enough to do this. But I'd already enrolled. And I couldn't back out now. I couldn't disappoint my parents.

"I already enrolled," I told him. "I have to start the classes."

I WORKED HARD TO FINISH my community college classes while working full time for my dad, and I applied to Spring Arbor University with plans to attend their satellite university fifteen minutes from our home. Upon my acceptance, I found out I'd have to attend their main campus—a forty-five-minute drive from our home—three or four days a week for the next two years.

Shocked, I broke the news to my mom. "I don't think I can do this anymore. They want me to drive forty-five minutes to class. Like three or four days a week."

"Okay," she said.

What the hell did she mean, *okay*?

"What? Okay, are you serious? I'm working full time. I can't drive that far. What will I do about the boys?"

"Rich is home, so he can take care of the boys after school. He can make dinner. You can work part time or quit. You're going to finish school because that's your goal, and it's something you started. Jodi, your boys are watching you, and they need to see you finish this," she said.

Years of arguing with my husband and agreeing to things I didn't want had worn me thin, but this was different. This was choosing to do something for me.

"Okay. I will. I'll do it. But are you sure?" I needed reassurance that I was enough, that I could handle the challenge.

"Yes, I'm sure. Your dad is sure," her voice was steady, certain.

"Okay, I'll get registered and let you know what days I'm going." The butterflies in my stomach caught in my throat, and tears welled in my eyes.

"Love you," she pressed.

"Love you, too," I whispered.

I WAS IN COLLEGE WHEN the dot.com bubble burst and the economy in Michigan took a slide. Being a tradesman, Rich was laid off, then unemployed. He was unemployed for the final two years of my college experience.

A diligent student, I did my homework in the evenings while helping the boys with theirs. Rich made meals and helped with their homework as often as I did. They loved being home with their dad and built a strong relationship with him. They particularly adored surprise trips in our Jeep with the top down.

"Boys, we're going for an ice-cream run," Rich announced one night after we'd already put the boys in their pajamas.

"Yay! I'm getting double chocolate," Phillip told Rich, grinning from ear to ear.

"Let's get your slippers," I said, jogging up the steps to their bedroom.

Rich took off the top of the Jeep, and we headed to Kilwins in East Lansing. It was our favorite spot to grab ice cream. Rich had worked on the building when it was built and had gotten to know the employees. He'd taken the boys there immediately after it opened, and the workers enjoyed seeing the boys eating ice cream in their pajamas. We took the roads between Holt and East Lansing because the boys felt like a part of the Michigan State University campus, waving to the college students on our drive. We needed to start earning some money.

IT WAS MY FINAL DRIVE down this long stretch of US-127, the four-lane freeway taking me through the rural area between my home and Spring Arbor University. I'd finished my degree, and this was my final drive to stand with my peers and collect my diploma.

The boys rode in the back of the car, and Rich sat next to me in the passenger seat. Nervous and apprehensive, I asked the boys, "Do you think you'll cheer for me?"

"Of course, Mom." Phillip, now in seventh grade, answered me in his manner-of-fact way.

The boys were inseparable. Neal quickly took to Phillip's friend groups, surrounding himself with Phillip's friends as often as he did his own. The boys rode their bikes around the neighborhood for hours. Neal matured quickly, and whether I liked it or not, he picked up the older boys' attitudes.

"You know, you earned this degree as much as I did," I said. "You boys sacrificed your time with me, helped me make dinners during the week, and sometimes even attended classes with me, so this is your degree too."

"No way! I don't want to teach. I don't even like little kids," Neal said. He'd just finished fourth grade and wasn't interested in children younger than himself.

Rich sat quietly. I knew he wasn't fond of my driving and was reserving his comments. I could feel the tension. I turned up the radio to drown out my stress. I didn't mention that he was instrumental in me earning my degree.

Arriving on campus, I saw Carrie, Shannon, and Sarah's cars—three women who, like me, were also mothers that made time for both school and work. They'd become my lifeline when classes and life became difficult. I ran into the athletic center foyer and gathered each of them into a hug. This would be our last time together on campus.

With our caps in hand, we congratulated each other and introduced one another to our families. Shannon had brought us each a small decoration to adorn our caps, a small memento for graduating together.

Pride swelled in my chest. I was the first of my immediate family to graduate from college. This had been my parents' goal for me for as long as I could remember, and I'd finally fulfilled their dream. I had successfully completed my undergraduate degree in elementary education with minors in social studies and language arts.

I sat with my classmates as the officials called out the graduates' names. My back was sore, and my head was beginning to ache, but this was my day. I pushed the migraine aside. I'd take some medicine and sleep when I got home.

Walking across the stage, I smiled at my parents, grandmother, brother, husband, and children. I heard their shouts and yells. My heart filled with pride. I'd done something well. I'd completed this goal without giving up and proved to myself and others that I was not a quitter.

It was one of the happiest days of my life.

I was excited to change the lives of students, improve their worlds, and help them like my teachers had helped me. But I was woefully unaware of the difference between the education system I had graduated *into* and the elementary education system I had graduated *from*. I had graduated from a network of teachers who cared about their students, visited students' homes when they were ill for a prolonged period, teachers who made learning fun rather than simply teaching to the test, and reinforced positive character traits. But I graduated *into* a system that focused on student achievement through standardized testing yet had unequal access to materials, unsafe schools, and a politicized system that believed teachers could resolve character traits that parents didn't teach at home.

"I GOT A TEACHING JOB! I'll be teaching seventh graders in the fall," I told my dad as I entered his office.

"Jo, that's great! Where is it?"

I'd dreaded this question. "North Carolina. We have to leave in a week. Rich got a job too. He hasn't worked in a year, and we can't live like this anymore. If we can't make it here at home, we must go somewhere else."

"What about the boys?" he asked. His face turned grim. The boys were as much a part of his world as they were my own. They spent weekends together when Dad wasn't golfing with his buddies. When we went up to the cottage, they were his little companions. They longed to be like him; in fact, all three of us did. We emulated Dad's behavior, his moods, and his actions.

"They're our kids, so of course we're taking them with us. They're moving." I tried to break it to him gently.

"Jodi. No, you can't take the boys," he said. Tears welled in his eyes.

Maybe I shouldn't have told him at work, but I felt protected from his anger in a semi-public space. Quietly, I shut the door to give us some privacy. Dad was used to being in control. He'd just moved into a beautiful new office space, and his business was bustling with new employees and business, outpacing its previous growth. He wasn't expecting this blow. He was normally the one telling everyone else how things would be.

"I didn't have a choice, Dad. Schools have already hired for the fall. There's nowhere else to go. Rich doesn't have any prospects in Michigan. We can't go another year with him not working. I had to find something. Maybe when I get some experience, we can come back, but I'm hoping we can build a better life for ourselves in North Carolina. Since we'll both have jobs, Rich has decided that we can buy a house." I was pleading with my dad to believe in me. Pleading with him to support this decision. Trying to believe it was the right decision myself.

He was silent for a moment, then said, "If you've already committed, I guess you'll go. I don't have to like it, though," he said. With a wave of his hand, he said, "I have phone calls to make," and he picked up the phone. I'd been dismissed.

My head and heart ached equally. Again, I'd disappointed my father. How could I make this right? I was always sitting on the fence, caught between my parents and Rich, never able to please any of them.

I stopped in my brother's office for a quick hug. I waited a moment until he hung up the phone.

"How'd it go?" he asked.

"Horrible. Just like we knew it would. You know Dad." It was my turn for the tears.

"Jo, it'll be okay. I'm kinda busy, but I'll see you later?" He offered a quick hug and picked up his phone.

IT SEEMED LIKE PHILLIP AND NEAL'S childhood flew by in an instant. They'd grown from toddlers with chubby, sticky fingers that handled books and puzzle pieces into tall soccer players who passed the ball up the field to their teammates.

I'd matured tremendously and was fiercely protective of my boys, always eager to learn from other mothers. Longing to fit in, early on, I'd surrounded myself with a group of moms in Michigan with the same-aged children. They had boys with similar interests, and we found that our lives resembled one another's in many ways. When the children were younger, we babysat for one another.

"Hi! Yes, the boys have just been playing," I said to Marianne. "They're fine. Please don't rush."

"I'll be there about 5:30. Sorry I'm running late, really," she answered. Like me, running to get groceries and doing errands without kids was a luxury.

"Seriously, don't rush. The boys are all playing outside. I'll see you when you get here. Love ya, girl." I really had grown to love my best friend like a sister. It was the relationship I'd longed for since childhood.

This friendship meant more to me than most others in my life. Marianne had helped me guide my children through their formative years, during elementary school while I went to college full time and struggled with my marriage. I didn't know how I was going to tell her we were moving. Avoidance was my normal mode of operation.

Rich was outside playing with the kids and came in for a glass of water. "Marianne will be here about 5:30. I guess you ought to tell Tony too."

Tony was Marianne's husband and had come to be Rich's best friend. The four of us were often together.

"Jo, it will be okay. The boys will adjust. You'll adjust." He tried to comfort me with his words, but they didn't provide me the reassurance I needed.

"I know. Part of me is excited, and the other is scared shitless. What will we do without friends or family? This is my world. North Carolina is beautiful. I can't wait to teach. I haven't found a job here . . . I must take care of our family . . . I can't do this alone. Things have to change if we move. You know I can't shoulder the financial pressures by myself anymore."

"Jodi, I'll follow you to the ends of the earth. We both have jobs waiting, and we'll buy a house. I promise you."

What he meant as reassuring words were empty to my heart that had been broken time and time again. I felt like I was looking down the barrel of a shotgun.

Telling Marianne and her family we were moving was one of the hardest things I've ever done. Flashbacks of third grade came to mind. Losing friends wasn't easy for me. How would I make new ones? Suddenly, none of this move felt right, and I questioned every detail of the decision. I had devastated my parents, my friends, my children, and most of all, myself. I didn't want to move, but I had to in order to provide for my children.

The moving truck would be here next week. That's when I'd rip off the Band-Aid.

9

MOVING FORWARD

N orth Carolina felt like another planet. There were different crops in the fields, and it felt like the drive from my rural home to civilization took forever. Soon I was meeting teachers and students.

"Yes, ma'am," Trenton answered, eyes cast down. I was on hallway duty with some other teachers.

"Honey, look at me when you talk to me, and you don't have to say ma'am." I smiled at this sweet young man who'd become one of my favorites.

Quietly, another teacher addressed me by my married name. "Mrs. Addiss, you know it's a sign of respect in the South to look down and say ma'am. Please don't discourage that behavior. Your own boys will need to learn this as well."

"Oh, I didn't know. Sorry." I felt like a reprimanded child. I'd left the friendly Midwest, where a warm greeting had to be replaced with proper Southern manners. There was so much to learn about this new culture, this new world.

Growing up near a college campus, I was accustomed to a mix of international students and a community of various colors and races. This new community seemed completely homogeneous. The stark reality of racial division caused tension, fear, and distrust in me. My curiosity wasn't welcome in Clayton, the small town where I lived, and certainly not in Micro, where I taught—a small community with a population of approximately 450.

Museums, basketball, and football games I once frequented at home in Michigan were now an hour away in Raleigh, and my students knew very little about them. Apple orchards were replaced with tobacco fields, my local grocery stores with a big boxy Walmart, paved roads with dirt roads and gravel. My daily commute to the school was along the dirt-stitched cotton and tobacco fields, the quilt of my surroundings.

The children I taught were nothing like the middle-class boys and girls I'd left behind. They often struggled, and I saw the evidence of the painful homes where many of them lived. Their lives triggered my trauma. I longed to rescue each of them, which was a problem. I attempted to rescue my students, family, and friends. If they didn't see their problem or weren't interested in a solution, I saw it as a failure on my part. I began creating a mental list of those failures, cracks within the facade I'd built around myself.

The excitement of our move wore off faster than we could unpack our boxes. The boys were quick to make friends, fit in with peers, and landed positions on a variety of soccer teams. Traveling with these teams was so different than what we'd left behind. Rich and I finally forged strong bonds with the families of two other players, and we shared our Thanksgiving with them, spent many evenings together, and became closely bonded. I relied on these moms, but the strong sense of abandonment I carried from my past was always a pervasive shadow within.

But the group of moms I'd left behind in Michigan couldn't be replaced. These new women were different. Along with those who had proper Southern personalities, there were some transplants—cautious, skeptical, gregarious personalities from New York and New Jersey. It was the East Coast woman with whom I found kinship. My previous coping method of mirroring other people's emotions wasn't easy in my new surroundings, and fitting into this new world became a daily struggle.

I no longer confided in Boo-Boo, and I withheld my emotions from others, afraid that sharing them would make them real. Finally, when the pain became unbearable, I lashed out at my family. Overwhelmed by guilt, I then begged for forgiveness. It was a vicious cycle.

Patterns from middle school emerged once again. I allowed others to speak to me disrespectfully. Lacking assertiveness, I became passive and compliant. In a misguided effort to put the needs and wants of others first, I began to self-sacrifice. I thought that I had to make everyone else's needs and wants my priority. I grew angry and resentful. I minimized myself in an effort to please others by taking on all our challenges.

My friendly Midwestern personality now completely closed off, I couldn't keep track of all the behavior expectations, strict rules, and proper personalities. I left my middle school teaching job and transferred to elementary, hoping for a change, but the struggle continued. Even the boys became frustrated with my struggle. We were at a crossroads.

"Rich, please, we need to go back home. I need to go back. The boys need to go back. This is not a good situation for us." It wasn't my first plea to fall on his deaf ears.

"There's nothing back in Michigan, Jodi. Your parents sold the house, so we have nowhere to live. I don't have a job there, and neither do you. The boys have been away from their friends and aren't interested in going back. I've asked them."

Every time I talked to Rich, he repeated the same excuses. I watched as he poured the amber liquid over the ice in his glass. Jim Beam and Coke. It had always been his favorite drink, and he drank it more frequently now.

"We need to move to an apartment in Apex since we both work there now," he said. "Let's get out of this house and find a different place."

"You promised we'd buy a house if we rented this one for two years. What happened to that promise, Rich?" I asked. "I'm tired of renting. We're just throwing money away. If you don't want to go back home, then I'll go. I'll take the kids and go." This wasn't the first time I'd made that threat.

"Seriously, you want a divorce? After everything we've been through? I've done so much for you. I was there for your migraines and seizures. I supported you through college, told you I'd follow you when you wanted to teach. Now you want to leave me? You can't take the boys. They won't go with you. You won't last a second without me!" he shouted.

It was late, and I was tired—tired of fighting, tired of living life on the edge. I wanted peace, happiness. I wanted to be back in Michigan with my boys, my family, and my friends. I wanted to resume a sense of normalcy—whatever that looked like.

"The boys have been unhappy since we moved," I said. "They fit in right away, but it's gotten hard. I hate it here. We've made some great friends, but all our real friends are in Michigan. Our family is there. I'll move to Apex for a year, but if things don't work, then I'm moving. I can't do this anymore. My migraines are out of control, and the doctors don't know how to fix them. I hate teaching, and seriously, I just need to go home. I'll keep trying for you, but I just want to quit and go home." I begged Rich, hoping to change his mind, hoping he would see or hear me, but he moved to the couch and turned on the TV to drown out the noise of my voice.

"Jodi, I said to stop threatening me. We'll move to Apex, and we'll make it work. We always do," he said, dismissing me.

Just like that, he halted the conversation. He made all the decisions. I was simply along for the ride, the kids and me. I just wanted it all to quit. Quit living in North Carolina and quit my life.

But I wasn't a quitter. I didn't quit when medical trauma shattered my world or when I was singled out by peers in middle school. This wasn't the first time I'd felt isolated and alone. When my boys were young, I'd glimpsed a peaceful, happy life, but now, I felt like I was in the midst of another traumatic battle, a war for my safety. My trauma had shown me I was a problem solver, however tired I was physically, emotionally, or spiritually. I did what I did best and continued the struggle.

No, I wouldn't quit. I would give him a year, two at the most. Rich would have to work with me, stop working against me, help put us on the right track, and put our family first. He would have to help put our finances and life back together if he wanted to make our marriage work. If not, I would put my foot down and tell him I wanted a divorce and follow through with it.

I had to tell my parents. I needed their support if I was going to keep my word to myself. Headed to Florida in a few weeks for spring break, I would ask them to help me come up with a plan.

THE HOT AIR HIT MY FACE as I watched numerous families and kids step off the plane ahead of me. The Florida humidity was a welcome reprieve, as was a week with Mom and Dad at their Florida home. Neal was still in high school, and Phillip was taking classes at the local community college. I was teaching at a year-round school, so we all had different spring breaks and earned separate weeks with Mom and Dad. It was like my reward for time served with Rich, but I certainly couldn't say that to my parents. Their thirty-year marriage served as an inspiration to family and friends, and I didn't know how they'd react to this blow of disappointment, another failure of mine.

Making my way toward the exit, I daydreamed about when Phillip and Neal were young. Our trip to the Grand Canyon was always present in my mind. The boys and I had taken a cross-country road trip with my brother Adam and

Mom and Dad. My mom's brother and his family joined us. My Uncle Doug and Aunt Michele's children—Jordan, Kyle, and Nicole—were about the same ages as Phillip and Neal. These were their closest cousins.

We piled into Uncle Doug and Aunt Michele's motor home and drove west. When we stood at the edge of the Grand Canyon, the kids stared into the amazing new world. Arriving at the canyon was like a spiritual connection. We were overwhelmed by its majestic beauty.

Staying in a hotel on the edge of the canyon, we witnessed the majestic splendor of its sunrise. We ate our breakfast on its ledge, watching the California condor sweeping and scavenging for breakfast of its own. Dad was in awe of the bird's magnificent wingspan, sitting each of the boys on his lap for quiet periods as they just watched and enjoyed one another's company. As the memories flooded back, I knew I needed to go home. I needed to build such memories again with my parents and children.

As I stepped out of the airport door, Mom and Dad both rushed in with hugs and hellos. It had been months since we'd seen one another. Our time apart had been difficult. Dad grabbed my bag and threw it in the back of the car.

"We can head over to lunch and then back over to the island, okay?" Dad was always excited to share fish baskets for our first island lunch.

"Sounds like a perfect day in paradise," I said from the back seat. The stress of my life lifted off my shoulders as I saw my parents' hands clasped together on the front armrest.

The next few days were pure bliss spent in the sun, island hopping for lunch on friends' boats, and swimming in the afternoons. Late one afternoon, I opened up. Dad and I were floating in the blue pool, and Mom was lying poolside when it burst out of me.

"I want to get a divorce."

A look of uncertainty passed between them. Mom spoke first. "Now? Jodi, are you sure?"

"Well, not right now, like today. But I think I've hit that point. I'm ready to come back to Michigan, and I don't think Rich wants to." I looked at Dad, trying to gauge his response.

"You know I'll support whatever decision you make," he said, trying to hold back his emotions. "How much do the boys know?"

"I haven't told them anything, and I don't plan on telling them until Rich and I make some final decisions." I made that perfectly clear to my parents. I didn't want them to mention anything to the boys.

"Okay. So, what do you need us to do?" Dad asked.

"I don't know." I glanced at Mom. "You know I'm not happy teaching. I think I want to get my master's degree from Michigan State in management, strategy, and leadership and come back to work for you, Dad." I knew I had to walk on eggshells with this one.

"This is too much, Sis. You know I'd love to have you back at the agency, but you're talking about too much at once. Let me process this, and we can talk again when you come home in a few months for the summer." He floated to the edge of the pool, grabbed his glass, downed the clear liquid, then set it down again.

"Okay," I said. "At least you know where my mind is. I want to finish out this school year and probably work the next one." I wanted to give him my timeline and relieve his mind a little. I glanced at them both tentatively, waiting for Dad's response.

"You know we love you too, Sis. It's just a lot to take in. I'm proud of you, and I know you can do this." Dad smiled at me. I knew he was okay with my decision.

We toweled off and went to dinner to celebrate our last day in paradise.

I returned to Michigan that summer more eager than ever to discuss a plan with Mom and Dad. But as I started the conversation, Dad grabbed at his chest.

"Dad, what's wrong? Are you having chest pain?" This wasn't the first time I'd asked him about having chest pain, and my concern was growing.

"No, I told you it's nothing to worry about. It's a stretched muscle." His face wasn't very reassuring.

It was more important than ever for me to get back to Michigan permanently. My father had saved me, and I knew something was wrong with him; I needed to save him.

Dad agreed that I could return to work with him and Adam the next summer and enroll in a master's program at Michigan State University the following fall.

MY HEALTH DURING MY LAST YEAR in North Carolina was worse than in the previous four years that we'd lived there.

I lay on the living room couch with the blinds shut. The blanket warmed me, but the blood thumped the pillow beneath my head. This had become my routine. Wake up with a headache, go to bed with a headache. Day after day, every day, migraines.

My medications were changed, and they caused irritability, frustration, anger, and intense emotions. I refused to tell anyone that my symptoms were a result of migraines and medication changes. My unstable emotions and health created problems for me as a teacher and in my other relationships. I left teaching before the school year had even begun and, home alone, I grew more isolated than ever, alone with my migraines.

My physicians tried different treatment modalities, preventative and abortive medications, IV therapy, inpatient hospitalization. Nothing worked. They didn't have any answers for me. I felt hopeless.

I needed to leave North Carolina. I needed to be home. Michigan was home. My family was there, and I missed them desperately.

Rich and I continued to argue about moving. I begged and pleaded. He wanted to stay in North Carolina. Nothing had changed. He was happy with the way things were.

I just needed to wait until the summer, until Neal finished his school year, and then I could go.

Rich and I had many altercations that year, with my anxiety on the rise. Each decision he made upset me and threw me further into depression. I had stayed in this unhealthy marriage because of my financial insecurity. We were further in debt than I wanted to admit. I knew I'd take the burden of the debt with me, and I had to get smart about the choices I'd make. I had to work out an agreement with Rich so he'd help me financially when the boys moved with me. I couldn't support them by myself.

Now, thirty-nine years old, I took Boo-Boo off my closet shelf. "Hello, old friend. Nice to see you here." I dusted his worn head off. It had been years since I talked to him. "Life hasn't gotten much better since I was seven, twelve, or twenty. These old emotions of stress and anxiety are still here." I rubbed his soft fur between my fingers.

My two small chihuahuas joined us on the bed, where I'd taken up residence. They snuggled their tiny cream and brown bodies into my own. I'd brought them home a few months before when my therapist suggested I get an emotional support dog. Well, I'd brought one of them home a few months before. The other one had been Rich's idea. He'd gone back to get her the next day. I loved Penny just as much as I did Teddy, although she had a bit of a wild side and added to some of my anxiety. She was a whirlwind of a thing—tiny, rambunctious, and mischievous. But Teddy fit the description my therapist recommended for an emotional support animal. He was a calm presence and a welcome companion. The puppies were inseparable, and the mere thought of taking one back caused me overwhelming feelings of distress. Not to mention, I could never tell Rich.

"Boo-Boo, there are just so many things wrong in this relationship. Warning signs I missed from the beginning. I wanted a companion, but what I needed was to work on myself. Who I needed to love was *me*. I've gotten myself into quite a situation. How do I ask a man who's given me the greatest blessings in my life for a divorce? We've been through so much together. I've been with him longer than I was single. But I cannot do this to myself anymore. And I can't do this alone either." Tears streamed down my face, and my breath caught in my throat. "How am I going to tell Rich that I need his help? How can I guarantee that he'll help with the boys?"

I knew the boys needed their father emotionally and physically. If we were to divorce, I'd have to convince Rich to move to Michigan so he'd be close to the boys. If he wouldn't move, then he'd have to promise to visit them regularly. I wasn't sure he would compromise with me.

As a mother, I'd put my children's needs first, and I believed that having their father in our home was necessary. I felt torn. I believed Rich needed his children just as much as they needed him. But if I was going to start loving myself, I had to stop putting my husband ahead of me.

Phillip and Neal, now twenty and seventeen, knew the medical treatment I received in North Carolina was ineffective. They understood that I could receive more comprehensive medical care in Michigan, where I'd also be able to return to work and begin graduate school at Michigan State University. We'd told them Rich would follow when he found a job.

Rich and I talked about divorce multiple times before I left for Michigan in June. We agreed that we'd separate for a few months before making a permanent decision. In May, he helped me pack the house, and in June, we loaded the U-Haul for our move.

"Hey boys, can we please finish loading the U-Haul tonight?" I asked. The boys had been working hard alongside Rich and me all day. It was now dark, and I knew they were tired, but we needed to finish. I wanted to be on the road by 7:00 a.m., so we'd be back in Michigan at a decent hour.

I took most of the belongings in the house, leaving Rich with some pots and pans, bathroom supplies, and a bed. My heart hurt for him. I was taking our children, the dogs, and everything he held precious.

"Mom, this is the last time I'm helping you move." Neal's feet pounded up the cement steps.

I knew he was serious. This was the fourth time he'd helped us move, and he was tired. Just as tired and worn out as I was.

Phillip shot me a look before catching up with his brother. If Neal was upset, then so was he. They had a strong bond. When one was pissed, so was the other, and that's how it was tonight.

They'll be really pissed, I thought, *when they find out about Rich and me.* But I pushed that thought out of my head like the thousand others that raced through it. We'd decided to tell them about our separation in Michigan before Rich returned to North Carolina. I couldn't see my part in the failure of this relationship. I would have other failed relationships before I understood.

The boys and I moved into a rental home in June 2014.

10

SEEKING RELIEF

A warm September wind blew through the window of my bedroom as I got ready for bed. It was the end of summer, and I appreciated every warm day and evening we still had. It was the first bedroom I'd had to myself since childhood.

"What the fuck?!" Neal stormed into my bedroom.

"What? Neal, it's almost 9:00 p.m. What's going on?" I didn't know what would make him so angry. Of the two boys, he was more laid back and slower to anger.

"You're getting divorced? Dad just called and told me." His face was red with rage. I sat on my bed and tried to put my thoughts together. I hadn't heard from Rich in a month. Whenever I called, I got his voicemail. He never returned my texts. I'd even called multiple hospitals in North Carolina, wondering if he'd been injured or was sick.

"Dad called you? I've been worried about him. I haven't heard from him in weeks." I didn't know what else to say.

"Yeah, he called me and Phil. You knew you were getting divorced when we moved back here in June, didn't you?" he pushed.

"Yes. We were going to tell you then, but when we got here, your dad didn't want to. And then he was gone, and I didn't know what to say. Neal, I'm sorry. I love your dad; I'm just not *in love* with him anymore." My tears started to flow, and my puppies came out from under the blankets.

"Whatever," Neal replied. "I need to go out and get something to eat." He walked out the door, pulling it shut behind him.

Rich hadn't called or seen the boys in months. He finally returned to Michigan and was living with different friends as he moved from house to house. He was unemployed, drinking, and his actions left our boys confused.

He started dating a woman who began threatening me on social media. Soon, Rich reached out and threatened me. Finally, I put a personal protection order in place. Our divorce was finalized in September 2018.

I realized how much I had stripped away from this man I once loved. Our children. Our family. Our belongings. Our life. I had failed him. I had failed my children. I felt responsible for Rich's problems that had intensified during our separation. I felt guilty for not giving people what they needed and not being able to resolve their problems—Dad, Mom, Rich, Phillip, Neal. The count was stacking up.

"COME ON IN, JO." Dad smiled up at me from over his desk. "It's good to have you back." It was my first day back at the insurance agency, and I was excited to meet the team that had amassed while I was gone.

Dad, Adam, and I had agreed that I would come back to work in the commercial lines department while I earned my management, strategy, and leadership master's degree from Michigan State University. Dad would start the work to transition Adam and me into ownership positions when he retired.

I tried to pull my life together as I worked alongside Dad and Adam, but my personal life continued to fall apart. My family saw it, then the employees saw it too. Shame, rage, and pain filled my daily life as migraines, which had been so out of control in North Carolina, didn't improve in Michigan. I anguished to find a physician who could treat my migraines, ached to find the right treatment.

The physical pain left my body in a constant, heightened state of fear, stress, and danger. I felt on edge and refused to tell anyone about my feelings. I alternated between stages of flight, fight, and freeze defense responses. My body and mind felt out of control. Something was terribly wrong.

THE NURSE DIMMED THE LIGHTS, but they were still too bright as I lay on yet another exam table. Curled in the fetal position, my reptilian brain had taken over. My heart raced in my chest. I tried to control my breathing and slow my heart rate. I'd sought help from numerous physicians and was tired of telling my story. I felt judged, overwhelmed.

Blood rushed to my ears. I could hear each sound—papers shuffling, the printer in the office, patients in the waiting room. I had to fight the feeling of running. I focused on my mom, who had driven me an hour and a half to the Detroit area. She would be what held me fast in this room and kept me grounded as I told my story and pleaded for help.

Pain Recovery Solutions pounded in my head. *Pain Recovery Solutions*—the name of yet another new doctor's office. I needed to recover from this pain. I needed a solution. I prayed for help.

"No one cares if I live or die from this pain. I can't take it anymore. I don't care anymore." Tears streamed as I described my situation to yet another nurse practitioner, Liz. Desperate, I looked to her for help, for solutions.

"We do care and have great treatment options. Did Dr. Cooper refer you to us?" she asked.

"No, I found you because I've tried everyone else in Lansing, and I'm out of options," I answered.

"Okay, I am going to make some phone calls, but I want to refer you to Dr. Cooper at the University of Michigan. He's amazing and will work with us as a team," she continued. "Can you come back next week for your first treatment?"

I looked over at Mom. "Can you drive me?" I asked.

Mom and Dad had been living in my spare bedroom three or four days a week, so Dad could continue his work at the office. They'd sold their home years ago and spent the rest of their time at their cottage, two hours away.

"Of course," she answered gently, always the caregiver. My caregiver.

It was the first time since returning to Michigan that any medical professional had offered me hope.

"JODI!" THE NURSE CALLED ME from the waiting room.

I walked with Mom into another exam room with this tall, blonde nurse. The University of Michigan had a different feel altogether, not what I was used to. The tall, brick buildings were professional and corporate, yet inside, the nurse reassured me that I would be treated with dignity and care. Those words—I'd heard them before, and it would take a world of commitment to win my trust.

"Your blood pressure's a little high, but that's probably because you're seeing a new physician today. Let's take it again at the end of your appointment." The nurse's kind eyes were not lost on me. It was an unusual change. My blood pressure was never high, but for a nurse to check it after my appointment was impressive and something that I'd not experienced before. I wasn't going to be won over quite yet, but I noticed that she went above and beyond.

Dr. Cooper went over my medical history, completed a neurological exam, and began to dig into my migraine treatment. He picked up my list of medications to review with me.

"Which of these have you found the most success with?" he asked.

"None. I've taken a lot. I checked them on the list, but I actually can't remember them all. There've been so many medications the last twenty years." I had listed more than twenty tried and failed migraine medications. Dr. Cooper and his nurse practitioner, Johanna, listened patiently, recording each tried and failed attempt in my electronic medical record.

"It's okay if you don't remember the names. Sometimes we're just looking to see if a certain type worked for you, like a triptan or a beta-blocker," Dr. Cooper explained. "If you have tried a few from the same category, then we know that that type of medication usually doesn't work for you, and we need to try a different treatment modality."

I continued to list the different unsuccessful treatments I had tried to relieve my now-daily migraines. Over-the-counter medications, a daily regimen of vitamins, what felt like thousands of prescriptions, biofeedback, acupuncture, massage therapy, chiropractic adjustments, electrical stimulation devices, counseling. The list continued.

"Continue with the daily sublinguals Liz has prescribed. I'm going to add a preventative and want you to have rescue medication on hand for any breakthrough headaches. Our treatment goal should be to give you 70 percent relief at this time." Dr. Cooper discussed a few possibilities for breakthrough migraines.

"Come back and meet with Johanna in two weeks. If you don't see any progress before then, I want to know. Message us on the patient portal," Dr. Cooper said.

For the second time in two months, I had hope that my migraines were going to be controlled. I wasn't sure how, but I trusted that these professionals would provide me with the keys to success.

Still, I was often a no-show to work due to the intensity of the migraines and the changes in medications and treatment. My family and staff were irritated and short-tempered with me. I didn't understand why they were upset. My brain was scattered. I couldn't see the workload I left behind, could not see beyond my pain.

Mom had taken me to my first few appointments in Detroit, but after that, I made the grueling ninety-minute drive by myself every other week with the very real belief that they would help. I knew that once I could trust these individuals and let them into my world, they would be able to help me.

After the long drive, I was always mentally and physically exhausted, immobilized by the hyper-aroused state I was stuck in. The pain of my migraines glossed over, and I dissociated from my experiences. Each visit sounded like the last.

"Um, I think this has helped my migraines, but I don't really know . . ."

"I hurt so bad; I can't really keep track . . ."

"I tried to write them down but lost my list and forgot because the pain was so bad . . ."

"I just want to sleep because of the meds . . ."

I fell back into old patterns. Paralyzed by fear, my memory failed me and went blank. Unconsciously, the years of trauma I'd experienced built up and were triggered daily, and I felt like I was repeating the past. The shame was overwhelming. Without answers for the doctors, I couldn't help myself. Here was a team of physicians willing to give me the answers and help me fix my life, yet I had closed them off, afraid of sharing my truth, afraid of revealing my innermost self. I was afraid that if I told them their treatment didn't help, they would discharge me from their care. They would leave me like friends had left me behind in childhood.

I began seeing a therapist who helped me see that my pain was connected to my trauma. I began confiding in my physicians and trusting their judgment. I found apps to track my migraines, their triggers, the symptoms, the medications I took, and the ones that worked and the ones that didn't. I began researching new medications on the market, new treatment modalities.

Alone, I couldn't control my treatment, but with a team of professionals, I could regroup my life. Working with experts, I could rebuild a life I loved.

THE DEER LOOKED PEACEFUL, walking in the woods outside the office window. I snuck in a few seconds of daydreaming before I picked up the phone to return the voicemails I'd received over lunch.

I loved working in the commercial lines department at the agency and the different types of insurance—liability, property, workers compensation, auto, and professional liability. I was always looking for new niche markets with the goal of continuing to build the business like my father, who'd found a niche market and doubled the size of his business.

I continued to work at the agency and go to school as I focused on my future. On this Saturday, I had my home-work completed by 2:00 p.m. I should have wanted to go out with friends to see a movie or go for a walk or head to the park—anything except falling into bed. But all I wanted to do was sleep for the rest of the weekend. Because I was emotionally and physically exhausted, I had no social life. I had nothing to give anyone, even myself. Self-care had gone by the wayside.

I found my favorite pajamas, slipped on the bottoms and the top, pulled back my comforter, and crawled between the sheets. Teddy and Penny had already warmed the area and snuggled quickly into my body.

"I don't have any energy. I don't have anything left to give anyone," I mumbled to these little puppies who had replaced Boo-Boo as my confidant.

Closing my eyes, I rested peacefully until Neal came in with some fast food, attempting to refuel me at dinner.

"Thank you, Son." Tears in my eyes, I looked up at him.

"Mom, you have to take care of yourself," he prodded me, aware of my circumstances. "You have to at least eat every day, three times a day."

"I know you're right, but sometimes I don't even have the energy to do that." I was ashamed to admit this, to myself, to my son.

"You need to talk to your doctors. Tell them." Neal was logical, unemotional. "Promise me. When's your next appointment?"

"I think it's next week. Maybe the following, but I will. I will tell them," I said. I would follow through. I would do anything for my children. I hated for them to see me like this.

"Okay, well, goodnight." He gave the puppies another pat, turned off my light, and shut the door.

I fluffed my pillow, raised the sheets for the dogs to climb back into their warm spots, and went to sleep. I would get up tomorrow and try to eat three meals.

IN JULY 2016, WE FOUND OUT that Dad had liver and kidney failure. Our worlds shattered. This man who supported our family, built us up, and built a flourishing business was now failing. How had this happened as we watched? I felt responsible.

"His liver enzymes are high," his doctor said on yet another visit.

"But what does that mean? I don't understand the diagnosis or how to treat my dad."

I'd been pushing for answers for weeks now. Dad had been in and out of hospitals in Lansing, Grand Rapids, and Muskegon, and no one could tell me what was going on.

"At Muskegon, they told us he has liver failure. Is that what high liver enzymes mean?"

"Yes," she said.

"It would have been easier for us to discuss and address this if you would have just said that the first time. Then we could have talked about it as a family and figured out what to do."

I was furious. Furious at the medical system for not being able to diagnose Dad, furious at my dad for letting it get this far, furious at the world. It had been a long time since I felt this intense rage.

After his diagnosis, Dad was often admitted to the hospital in extremely fragile health. We all longed to spend this precious time with my father. My boys and I would spend hours at his bedside. Adam and his wife Elizabeth would find time to visit without their son, Connor, who couldn't tolerate long stretches at the hospital. Mom refused to leave his side. She was back in the caregiver role she'd known during my childhood, her trauma relived.

WHEN I MET ERIC ONLINE, my life was a whirlwind of turmoil. Side effects from tried and failed migraine medications were again racking my body, my father was terminally ill, and I was trying desperately to fix this. These inner traumas created a symphony of emotions that played out in my professional life in a negative and destructive way.

I'd purchased a new home in July, around the time my father was diagnosed with kidney and liver failure. Phillip, now twenty-one, and Neal, nineteen, were living in my home, and my parents were there full time too. The boys helped Mom and me take Dad to the hospital and dialysis center every other day. Our meals and diets changed according to my dad's needs, and life in general became distorted. I felt like I was looking through a different lens.

I'd completed my management, strategy, and leadership master's degree the previous June, and now that I was out of school, I thought that working full time would be a breeze. No more homework and classes! But it was anything but easy. My father was barely able to work, and the stress increased. The employees questioned what roles they would play in a now-changing agency. Adam and I found ourselves in heated disagreements, and I went from being excited and hopeful about what we could do with Dad and the agency to being concerned.

Eric came into my life in August 2016, three months before my father died. I believed that God had sent him to help me through the trials that were to come.

"I'M RUNNING ABOUT THIRTY MINUTES LATE. I'm so sorry, Eric." It was our first date, and like every other day that week, I pushed the speedometer over the limit posted. I couldn't even get somewhere on time!

Fitzgerald Park, or the Ledges, as we had called it growing up, felt like a perfect place to meet this new man who enjoyed running, rodeos, and skydiving. A walk along the river and 300-million-year-old rock formations seemed like the perfect way to get to know someone.

I'd raced home from work, thrown on a spaghetti-strapped tank and shorts, put my hair in a messy bun, and topped off my outfit with some glitter slip-ons. Adorable!

"It's okay," he said. "I'm just sitting here drinking some water and taking in nature. Don't rush." Eric sounded relaxed. His reassuring tone put me at ease, and I slowed my car, albeit slightly.

"Okay, see you soon. Bye." The butterflies fluttered in my stomach.

After a twenty-year failed marriage, I promised myself I would take my time. I knew that Eric was someone special, and love was a slow journey. We both came into the relationship hurt, apprehensive about starting over with someone new.

Eric had two boys from his previous relationship. He found co-parenting with the boys' mother stressful. I understood his caregiver role because I was in the same situation myself, caring for both my children and my father.

It was an emotionally overwhelming time, and I was grateful for Eric and the reprieve of a new relationship. It was an escape from my life. Eric's joy, happiness, laid-back attitude, and laughter were a bright addition to my world.

We were both excited to be with someone new, and our relationship was relaxed and easy. We spent as much time together as our schedules would allow; we lived thirty minutes apart, driveway to driveway. Eric had joint custody of his two children, Cody and Justin, then twelve and seven, respectively. We found that spending Wednesday, Thursday, and every other weekend together worked best.

We enjoyed relaxed days together, sitting quietly in restaurants, putt-putt golfing, and simply getting to know one another. Although I promised myself I would take the relationship slow, I allowed the urgency of dad's illness to rush its pace and quickly introduced Eric to my family.

One evening in late September, Eric and I decided to make stir-fry for my mom, dad, and the boys. The sun shone through the back patio door into my kitchen. It was a beautiful evening. The boys laughed with Eric.

"Did our mom tell you she cooks on a regular basis?" Neal shot Phillip a look. I knew the teasing that was coming. Cereal and toast were my specialties.

"No, she said she likes baking." Eric smiled at the boys.

"She hasn't baked since she was little!" Mom laughed.

"This is probably the first and last time you will see her cook," Neal laughed, "especially if it's something you want to eat." We all laughed.

In my family of amazing Italian cooks who could spin meals out of scratch, I'd never learned to cook. Eating was my specialty!

Eric mixed the vegetables into the stir-fry, and I glanced at Dad. He gave me a wink and a nod. I knew what that meant. It was okay to make my own decision on this one, something I'd never felt confident enough to do before. He knew he'd be gone before I was ready to make that decision.

I walked over to him and gave him a hug while he sat quietly in the kitchen chair. Dad had become frail. This rock of my life was becoming worn and tired. Normally gregarious and outgoing, Dad would have helped with the meal and spun chatty tales, wine glass in hand. Now he sat quietly, trying to conserve enough energy to get through dinner.

AT HOME AND WORK, I STRETCHED myself thinner and thinner. I was caring for an ill parent, was a new homeowner, helped Adam manage the office, juggled a new relationship, babysat my nephew Connor frequently, and still dealt with uncontrolled migraines. Above all, I tried to stop my dad from dying. It was only a matter of time before something snapped.

Work was the only place I felt like I could stay in control. I cared about the people in our office and felt responsible for the welfare of the business and its management. My personality grew more abrasive as I closed down emotionally. I thought the more I took on and controlled, the less I would think about my dad.

I was an innovative and transformative manager. Adam and I were setting a purpose and direction for the agency but had different ways of guiding teams and executing strategies.

After years of laisse-faire management, I took it upon myself to find solutions and guide employees as decisions makers, pushing them out of their comfort zones before they were ready. I moved too fast and spread myself too thin. Employees who were once peers and friends felt betrayed. They'd seen my father as family, his paternalistic management style rarely explained reasoning, but asked for loyalty and trust.

The more ill my father became, the more out of control I felt. The quicker I made decisions that were necessary to grow a business, the more abrasive my personality became. The constant dread in the pit of my stomach spun in the whirlwind which was now my personality.

"I'm sorry, Adam, I won't be in today." Another call, another day, another migraine. I was beyond frustrated.

I tried to keep my physical pain hidden, but it hindered my work, just as it had in North Carolina. The more stress I was under, the worse it became. My life was not going according to plan.

"Jo, this has to stop. What am I going to tell everyone? They're tired of picking up your workload." Adam was right to be upset and guilt sunk in my gut like a stone.

"I don't know. I'm in pain. I can't think. I'll try to be back tomorrow. It's not like I want to be this way." I pleaded with him to see my perspective, but I understood that he was trying to explain my absence to frustrated employees.

"Adam, I have to go. I need to take some medicine. I'm sorry. I'll check in later." I knew the medications weren't helping me attain a healthy, productive life. Some of the side effects of the migraine rescue meds left me fatigued, nauseous, weak, anxious, depressed, and with memory loss. Furthermore, they'd caused weight gain, trouble with my concentration, agitation, hyperactivity, depression, and a list of other behavioral changes. I never knew what to expect; no one else knew what to expect of me either.

"Whatever. Bye." The phone clicked in my ear. I knew Adam was upset. I knew employees were upset. Dad would be upset. I was upset. Here was another thing I couldn't do right. Just add it to the fucking list. I was so tired of making mistakes. So tired of being a screwup. I didn't think I would ever get it right.

Frustrated, mad, and anxious, I heaved my aching body out of bed. I needed something to eat, water, and some medication. I made my way downstairs to the refrigerator, pulled out the milk for a bowl of cereal, and grabbed a bottle of water. I took a handful of rescue medications out of my purse and poured them into my hand. Hopefully the food, water, and meds would take the edge off the pain.

I quickly ate, threw the pills back into my mouth, swallowed, and made my way back upstairs to crawl into bed.

IN THE FINAL DAYS THAT Dad struggled with kidney failure, Adam sat down with Mom, Dad, and me to express his concerns about the office. He spoke for thirty minutes while I tried to defend my point of view, but finally, I heard what my brother had said. Not only did he not want me there, but neither did the employees. I broke down, angry, frustrated, and confused. Fear of losing my dad mixed with my traumatic past.

I thought about my situation as I drove home from the senior living center where my parents had temporarily moved when Dad grew sicker. Stay and fight or give up? I was tired. Everything was always a fight.

And this felt so damn familiar—it felt like my past and the bullying I'd faced, being unable to explain myself, my parents unable to understand my perspective. I tossed and turned in my bed that night; Teddy and Penny snuggled tightly into their spots next to me. Tears flowed freely down my face.

I didn't want to fight anymore. I loved my brother, and I loved the agency, but I'd grown so weary over thirty years of health issues and emotional strain that I didn't have anything left to give. I had to step away from the agency I loved. Dad had always referred to the agency as a living being, as our sister. He'd raised her along with us. She became a living being. I was emotionally invested, attached, and I didn't know how to separate. Losing her was like losing a sibling.

My father was dying before my eyes, and I couldn't do anything. Now, I was losing the agency too. How could I step away while watching my father die? I knew I'd have to also walk away from my family when I left the agency. It would be too painful to stay and see the business grow without me.

Of course, I couldn't do it gracefully. I wasn't capable. I didn't know how. So, I did it the only way I knew how—with trauma, fear, anger, and frustration. It was clear that I was no longer an asset but a liability, and I had to walk away.

The next day, Adam and I met in our dad's office.

"If you want to talk to me about work, you cannot attack me personally," I told Adam.

Trauma already triggered, I dissociated before I even heard his answer. He resumed the conversation from the evening before.

I spilled my coffee across the table and walked out. Tensions high, I not only walked away from the agency but the relationships with my family.

I felt abandoned and alone.

11

THE UNTHINKABLE

Phillip was rebuilding a 1997 Jeep Wrangler, engine to frame. My garage was a mess, but he was determined to see this project completed, and he was determined to show us his capabilities. During the year it had taken, he'd faced the doubts of family and friends.

"Phillip, just give up. Clean up my garage, find a car, and park it in that spot," I said. "You don't have a mechanics degree, honey. You don't know what you're doing. You're wasting your time." It was after 11:00 p.m. I was tired and ready for bed, but the engine revved, and no one in the house could sleep, including my parents.

"Mom, I'm going to do this. I've followed lots of YouTube videos. All the parts are here. Just . . . whatever." He rolled his eyes and ducked back under the green square hood.

His friends filled the garage at odd hours to assist him with the project. I hoped their experience was something helpful.

I turned to Mom and said, "Apparently, it's going to be a bit longer. I can't get him to see reality, so I'm going to bed." I embraced Mom and peeked in on Dad, who was already asleep.

"Honey, it's going to be okay." Ever the diplomat, Mom tried to make peace between Phillip and me.

DAD WAS ADMITTED TO SPARROW HOSPITAL again and was receiving daily dialysis. Mom and I helped him to the edge of the bed and moved the seat near the window. It was no easy task but worth the effort. I knew the boys were at the top of the parking garage, just below his window. Phillip had finally finished his Jeep project.

"Okay, Dad. You comfortable?" I sat him up as well as possible. I knew each dialysis treatment was prolonging the inevitable, but I wasn't ready to let Dad go, not yet. My kids needed more time. I needed more time.

"Yeah." He certainly didn't look comfortable but tried to adjust himself among all the tubes.

I sent the text and heard the engine roar to life. It was so loud it shook the windows. Then Phillip honked the horn.

Dad's eyes filled with tears. "He did it?"

"Yep. He and Neal are down on the top of the parking garage right now. No mechanical degree, just time, effort, and dedication. You bought them that vehicle, and he refused to let it die." My eyes filled with tears, and he understood my meaning.

"I love those damn boys," was all he could choke out.

"Me too, Daddy, me too. Let's get you back in bed." I pushed the nurse's button, so she could help. Dad, now tired, would be difficult to get back in bed.

I'D SPENT THE NIGHT at Eric's house, too exhausted to drive home. It was a Thursday night. Eric and I planned on spending the weekend together. I would get up on Friday, stop at the hospital to check on my parents, stop at the house to check on the boys and puppies, and come back to his place.

The phone rang in the wee hours of the morning, and my heart dropped. Immediately, I knew something was wrong. I rushed out to the living room, where my phone was plugged in.

"Mom," I answered, tears running down my face.

"He's gone." She could barely get the words out. "I laid there next to him. Jodi, I don't know what to do," she choked out, sobbing.

"Are you going back to the apartment?" They had moved from my house to an assisted living apartment a few weeks earlier. I knew she wouldn't stay there and would be back at my home soon. The boys and I would take care of her until she was ready to go back up to their lake cottage.

"Yes. I just want to get some rest. I don't think I'll be able to sleep. I love you. Bye," she said, exhaustion filling her voice.

"Me either. I love you too. Bye, Mom." I hesitated to hang up. I was afraid it would make the situation real.

Eric walked into the room, and I turned, tears streaming down my face. Fear and panic registered at the overwhelming reality that I hadn't saved my father. I couldn't stop him from dying. Couldn't save my family from this overwhelming pain.

Eric took me in his arms and allowed me to cry. I couldn't remember falling asleep, but I woke the next morning with sore eyes and a headache. Confused, afraid, numb—I didn't know what I felt. My world was void. I didn't know how to live in a world without my father. He'd taught me how to keep going, how to put one foot in front of the other. He'd given me life, and I couldn't do the same for him. I didn't deserve to take another breath.

BECAUSE I HAD A PASSION for language and writing, Mom asked me to write my father's obituary. I didn't know how to explain the uninhibited, gregarious person my father was or write about his devotion to our family, the commitment to his profession and colleagues, and the love he found in sports and nature—all in a few short paragraphs. The task was overwhelming.

I cherished my relationship with my father and had no words for it; I could not explain our bond. I wrote about my childhood, our experiences, how he supported me, and my love and dedication to this man who hadn't left my side regardless of the flaws I saw within myself. Then I realized I'd written about *my* feelings. My feelings about him and our relationship. This was not an obituary—it was a journal of sorts. How would I live without him?

I heard the rhythmic tick . . . tock . . . tick of the clock on the living room mantle, a leftover from my failed marriage. Tears began to flow. I missed his hugs already. How long would I remember his voice? I tried to refocus and calm my nerves.

"Coffee. That will help," I said to the empty room. The puppies looked up but didn't respond.

I filled the machine with water, put in a pod, and pressed the button. Hot, steaming coffee flowed into my mug. I grabbed the creamer from the fridge, poured it in, and fell back into the kitchen chair. I took a sip, and it burned the inside of my mouth, so I took another drink. Made sure I felt something. Anything. I had to temporarily set aside my emotions and think rationally.

I stared down at the bright white page, glowing white. Was this the way climbers faced the chaos, snow, and icy white path into the sky-top summit of Mount Everest? It felt that difficult to me. I started with his personality traits. I wrote his name on the top of the sheet and listed the characteristics I loved about my father.

Love. Wisdom. Truth. Bravery. Respect. Discipline. Family. Protection.

Finally, the words began to flow, and they didn't stop. I grabbed more paper, three more sheets. The words made no sense. Strange, fragmented paragraphs. Random sentences. Word. Words, lots and lots of words. There were so many. When I only needed a few paragraphs.

I didn't know how to edit all these deeply emotional feelings.

I needed to tell people what a wonderful man my father was, not just write it. Maybe I would speak at his funeral. Pieces of these writings could serve as both his obituary and eulogy. But could I get up at his funeral and talk about him, tell people about this remarkable man who'd raised me? Yes, this was a way in which I could honor my father. I couldn't honor his business any longer, but I could honor his memory like this.

I met people at his wake whom I didn't know existed. They all had beautiful stories about Dad. Wonderful stories that I hadn't heard. Stories about his childhood, his teen years, hunting stories, stories of business trips taken around the globe. None of these people knew what it was like to be raised by this man. I would tell them what a powerful experience it was. What an amazing experience it was. How incredibly blessed and fortunate I was. How blessed my children were.

THE FUNERAL HOME DIRECTOR flagged Eric and me into the line at the funeral home. We would park, stay for the service, follow to the internment, and return to celebrate Dad's life.

The crisp November air had a cold bite. I wasn't prepared for my body to betray me, to enter a hypervigilant state as I walked through the doors.

The bright lights, people, music. It was too loud, too bright. Overwhelming. There were too many—too many variations, too many combinations, too many colors. The flowers overwhelmed my sense of smell. I was flooded with a sense of danger and wanted to fly out of there, but I fought to stay in a space that was supposed to bring me comfort.

My head throbbed and ached, my body responded as it never had before. It was in a full-blown trauma response. Thirty years of repressed trauma, my delayed response was now hyper-aroused. I tried to sit quietly, fearful of the crowd. The friends. The family. My mind knew it didn't make sense, but none of that mattered to my feelings.

I didn't understand what was happening to me. I misinterpreted the situation as dangerous. Somehow in my mind, it resembled my previous trauma. I had no control. I'd lost my father. I was connected to this life-and-death situation, and I'd failed to save him.

I'd committed to speaking at the service, and now I was flooded with shame and fear and wanted to back out. I had to push down these feelings. So, I did the only thing I knew how. I dissociated, blunted my emotional processing, drew within myself. At the podium, I was numb. The faces were blank, but I was determined to share my experiences and the privilege I felt by being raised by a man of unequaled measure.

TWO MONTHS. FOR TWO MONTHS, I lay on Eric's couch. Despondent. Depressed. I refused to answer my phone. I ate what he brought me. I completed basic hygiene tasks. I slept. I waited to stop breathing. The trauma of losing my dad triggered another trauma. I felt like I had no right to survive. I was in the hyperarousal stages of post-traumatic stress disorder and was unintentionally reliving previous events.

"Jodi, you have to get up today." Eric was persistent. He kept trying and kept loving me when I couldn't love myself.

He prompted me to go to the movies, hike nature trails, and he took me shopping in attempts to get me to resume normal life. He drove me to my appointments and made sure I took medication, communicated with my physicians. He was my lifeline.

"Here, babe, let's get you out of the house. Let's go get some coffee. You love coffee," he said as he guided me into the bathroom and opened the shower door for me to step into the hot, running water.

"No. I don't want to. I don't want to get dressed."

I'd never been this depressed. My father was my rock. Who would I look up to now? Who did I have to work for?

"Here, baby. The shampoo will feel good in your hair. Get in there, wash up, then get out and dressed. I'll get you some pajamas. You can at least come with me, and we'll go through the drive-thru." He was digging deep, doing his best to convince me.

"Okay."

The hot water felt good on my skin. I wanted it to peel off the layers of sadness that had built up over the last sixty days without my father, without my family.

I was still angry about the agency, and Adam and I still weren't speaking. Neal was living at home and working full time. My relationship with Mom was still strained over decisions about the agency ownership. I'd spoken to her only once or twice. I knew she was going to Florida for the winter season.

"PHILLIP, I'M NOT SURE THAT Jeep will make it to Florida. Please just buy a plane ticket, and we can work out a car when you get there, and you get a job."

He was determined to take his beloved Jeep to his Pop and Nan's house to help take care of his Nan the first winter after losing my dad.

"Mom, it will be fine," he answered. "If not, I have AAA, and they can tow me to a station. I can repair it and get back on the road. I already told Nan that I'm coming. I've looked for a job and talked to a couple of places."

His lighthearted spirit warmed mine, but the logical side of my brain was frustrated and weary. I finally gave in.

"Okay. Let me call AAA and make sure you're on the policy. Please don't leave without seeing me first. I'll text you, and we can make some dinner arrangements."

Mom and Dad had purchased a home in Florida three years earlier, and the boys enjoyed spending time with them at the beach as much as they did at their lake cottage. And Phillip was determined to make sure his nana was taken care of. She would have someone in the house to talk to, someone to help her with household jobs, and a companion. He refused to let go of his grandmother as much as he refused to let go of his grandfather's spirit.

"MOM, I GOT THE JOB!" Neal announced one evening.

Phillip had left for Florida a few months earlier, and Neal had applied for a big change as well. To my mama heart, this was too overwhelming, but I tried to show my enthusiasm.

"Neal, that's great! Tell me about it." I smiled.

"I'm leaving for New Jersey next week. I'll be installing solar!" He grinned from ear to ear. "I don't know when I'll be back, but they'll put me up in hotels, so you don't need to worry about that." He was exuberant.

"So, you're going to stay in hotels and travel. You don't know when you're coming home?" I felt abandoned.

I was overjoyed for my son, who was headed out on a new career path, but I hadn't envisioned him leaving my nest yet, and I mourned for myself. But he was level-headed, ready to tackle the world. I knew he was sure-footed and ready for the decisions ahead of him. I wanted to support him.

"Okay. Yes, it's going to be great, Neal. I love you." I reached up, giving him a hug.

"I love you, too, Mom." He hugged me squarely, and I realized that my son had not only outgrown me physically but also outgrown my home.

"I CAN'T BELIEVE it's been another year, Mom," I said. I'd been trying to repair our relationship and spoke to her on the phone more frequently.

"I know. It doesn't seem like it. I still miss him. Wait for his calls. Wait for him to walk in the door." I could hear her soft sobs. They matched my own.

"Have you thought about seeing a therapist?" I asked.

"No. I don't think I need therapy, but I know it's helping you. I'm so proud of you." Her smile reached through the phone like a warm hug.

"Whether it's helping depends on the week," I said, "and the effort I put into it. I'm still learning to trust. Still learning to unbox these emotions. It hurts."

It was the truth. These were the same emotions I'd given to Boo-Boo as a child—and over the course of my life. Emotions that were too big for my eight-year-old brain. Emotions I didn't know how to label or process pushed out, and I had never learned to label or process.

"I love you, Jodi," she said, the sadness in her voice heavy.

"Love you too, Mom. Talk to you tomorrow. Bye." My heart sunk. There was nothing I could do to take away her pain. My pain. My children's pain.

In therapy, I was dealing with survivor's guilt. The survivor's guilt that I'd buried after the accident, and now the guilt I felt because I couldn't save my father.

I was irritable, felt helpless, and lacked the motivation to find a job, see my family, or get off Eric's couch. When I wasn't numb to my feelings, I was anxious. My thoughts raced, and I wanted to escape my life, escape from everything and everyone around me.

I regretted that my aunt had picked me up thirty years ago, come and gotten me so I could be with my cousin, who I so deeply enjoyed being around. In my mind, the accident was my fault. If it weren't for my wants, my needs, the accident would never have occurred.

I regretted not coming to Michigan sooner, not finding the right doctors to treat my father, not knowing how to save his life. I believed that it had been my job to watch over my father, to predict this outcome and prevent it from occurring. Post-traumatic stress caused me to be on alert and look for situations where someone could get hurt. Frustration and self-blame became my default emotion when someone I loved got hurt in a situation over which I had no control. After the loss of my father, I felt like it was my fault that my family was suffering from this loss and grief.

I would ruminate day and night over the choices I'd made in my life. Things I could have done differently to change the circumstances or change the outcome. I dreamed of going back and fixing things. I dreamed of doing things over. I longed to fix the world I found myself in that was upside down and sideways.

I felt out of control emotionally, socially, physically, and spiritually. I gave up on myself, my friends, my family, and God.

But in November, a flyer came home from the elementary school looking for coaches.

> ## *Become a Coach, Change Her Life!*
>
> Inspire and empower girls by volunteering as a coach. Our girls need you more than ever! You do not need to be a runner; you simply need to have a desire to support and encourage girls.

I wasn't a runner, and I didn't know anything about *Girls on the Run*, but I was drawn to the words. I continued reading.

> **Looking for enthusiastic, dedicated, and positive volunteers who are committed to empowering girls with valuable life lessons:**
>
> - Receive all the tools and support you need to lead interactive and easy-to-follow lessons with your co-coaches
> - Help girls grow their confidence, stand up for themselves, and give back to their communities
> - Must have availability once or twice per week on weekday afternoons
> - Experience the positive impacts yourself

Before I even read the last lines of the flyer, I was hooked. Runner or not, I knew I could commit to making sure another little girl never felt like I did.

Among conversation, laughter, hugs, and energy awards, you will witness transformational change in the girls, and don't be surprised if you realize that you are positively changing as well. The program may end in 10 weeks, but for our coaches and girls, the finish line is just the beginning. Ready to make a difference and encourage girls to realize their full potential?

The eight-year-old girl I'd lost longed to be included in this team, these conversations, and the laughter, hugs, and energy.

I signed up immediately. This was just what I needed to jumpstart my life. Within a week, I received an email confirming what I already knew, that my background check had been approved.

Our first training session would be in February.

12

THE UNBEARABLE

M y eyes snapped open. I sat up, heart racing. The room was dark. I looked at Eric. "Was that the doorbell?"

"Yes." His heart now raced as rapidly as mine. I looked at my phone: 2:00 a.m.

The bright, white porch lights shined down on two uniformed Michigan State Police officers. Their faces loomed through the massive glass door that had drawn me into the home we'd purchased just nine months earlier.

I turned to Eric. This felt like a dream, and I needed to wake up. He urged me to open the door. Blankly, I disengaged the multipoint deadbolt meant for protection.

"Good evening, ma'am, sir. We hate to bother you this late at night. Are you Jodi Gilroy?"

"Um, yes. Can you tell me what this is about?" Fear rose in my gut, the room spun, nothing seemed right. Eric and his ex-wife had been in court over custody of their boys. I thought this had something to do with her.

"May we come in, please?" The woman officer was polite, kind.

"Yes." I backed away from the door.

"You should sit down." No, no, I would not sit down. Whatever was coming, I would stand. I could take it. Just tell me. My mind raced; my stomach churned.

"Jodi, honey. Here, sit at the table." Eric guided me to the table.

The officers didn't come any further. They stayed in the living room.

"Is your son Phillip Addiss? Does he live in Florida?"

"What? Yes? What's wrong? What happened?"

"There was an accident on Stringfellow Road. Does that sound familiar to you?" they continued.

"Yes, I know where that is. What . . . what happened . . . what?" I looked at Eric. Bile rose in my stomach. The rock in the pit of my stomach grew larger.

"I'm sorry, ma'am, but he passed away. We don't know all the details. We received a call from their dispatch, so we could come and let you know."

"What? No, are you sure it was my . . . " My voice broke off, and I sat there, shocked. Stunned. I had no words. Nothing. Empty. I felt like God could not take another person from me, but He had.

I tried to focus as the police continued to talk, providing me with information. Eric wrote down the information on a slip of paper. The team of officers left a business card and encouraged me to call them if I had any questions.

Questions flooded my mind, but there were none they could answer. I needed to talk to my mom. Their island was small, and I was sure she'd been contacted.

I didn't know what to say.

I had to call Neal. Again, I had no words. For the first time in my life, I was speechless.

News of Phillip's passing was on Facebook the next morning. Word on the island traveled quickly. His friends had found out and were devastated. They shared his memory the way young people do in this age—in public, on social media. My stomach lurched. I hadn't yet processed what had happened. I'd only talked to the two family members closest to me, yet social media made my son's death public.

My motherly instincts kicked into overdrive. I'd do everything I could to protect his memory. It was my job to share his light with the world.

I shared my first post:

My heart will never be the same. You changed me as a person, taught me what it means to love another before yourself. Loving a child is unlike any gift from God and having it ripped from my soul too soon is heartbreaking. Many of you know, my firstborn son, Phillip Addiss, was tragically taken from me in an accident on Wednesday night. I will spare you the details because they don't matter, and I still cannot process them.

Phillip was a bright shining light to anyone he met. He was kind and loving. Phillip was brilliant and insightful. There are not enough words to share the depth of his soul with this world.

Please share your photos and stories with us as we process this loss.

The next few days were a blur. There were parts of the day when I felt like I was stuck in a nightmare and others that I didn't realize had occurred.

I received my first phone call from Adam. He'd arranged our flight to Florida. We would go to Florida, meet with Mom, and he would bring Phillip's belongings home to Michigan. Mom and I would fly him home for services. I still couldn't process what was happening. Eric threw clothes into a suitcase for me and took me to the airport.

Mom picked us up. "Do you want to eat?" she asked. She had so much to say. "Have you heard from the funeral home regarding the flight back to Michigan? Have they booked his flight? I know you want to be on the same flight. We need to make sure we buy tickets on time.

"Jodi, we received these cards and flowers.

"Here's the card and message from the pastor and his wife."

For some reason, hearing that last sentence made me feel ready to go to the scene where my son took his last breath.

I crossed the gravel on the side of the road near the curved road sign on the hard-packed, brown dirt. I could see the dried blood left from my son's body. I laid my head next to it, my body racked with sobs.

I knew this was where his motorcycle had crashed. Phillip had wanted a motorcycle since childhood, and he realized that dream when he got to Florida and found the weather was prime for year-round riding. He took riding lessons, got his motorcycle license, found the Ducati dealership, and purchased his motorcycle in typical Phillip fashion—with much contemplation.

Adam and Mom stood near the sign, unsure of what to do or say. There was nothing they could say to relieve this pain, take away the need to find my son and take him home with me.

We found that Phillip had been taken to a funeral home, so they could make arrangements for his transportation back to the funeral home in Michigan. I refused to allow my son to fly alone. Delta Air Lines promised me that I could fly home with my child.

It took two days to make our flight plans and arrange a U-Haul to bring home Phillip's belongings. Adam would drive the U-haul, and Mom would fly to Michigan with me. As a team, we sorted through his belongings, the tools in the garage that he'd haphazardly stored, the dirty laundry that still smelled like him. I wanted to take it all, but most of all, I wanted my son. There was nothing that could replace his joyous light and chivalrous spirit.

THE OLDER GENTLEMAN LOOKED UP at the windows of the airport as I put my hand on the glass, watching them load my son into the belly of the plane. His face was kind, and he nodded toward me with respect. I knew that this wasn't the first time he'd done work of this nature. He was the leader of the crew that loaded the plane on what would be Phillip's final flight. I was grateful for this nameless man.

As we landed in Detroit, freezing sleet and icy cold winds rocked the plane as hard as my sobs. I called the funeral home again to verify that they had a car waiting to pick up Phillip from the airport.

OVER THE SUMMER, ERIC AND I needed to continue working on our wedding plans. We were planning a big ceremony in Jamaica, but that was before we lost Phillip. Eric had proposed to me the previous spring. We'd taken his boys to Disney World for spring break. Eric had arranged for my mom and her sister, my aunt Sherry, to meet us at the park, where he got down on one knee in front of the castle and asked me to marry him. I was elated, and my answer was an enthusiastic yes! We would be surrounded by family. Only now, there would be a hole.

I was stopped cold in February when Phillip died. Planning a wedding during my grief felt like a betrayal to my son; I felt like I could have one or the other, and I couldn't balance the emotions. I felt like I was being disloyal to Phillip and Dad if I didn't grieve nonstop.

After many conversations, Eric understood that I couldn't get married without both of my boys there, so we changed our plans. We'd have the wedding in Jamaica with only the couple who were standing up for us. It would be intimate and small. Rob and Mandy would come for the ceremony, and Eric and I would stay for our honeymoon. I began to see that to feel joy, I must experience pain. Eric and I had experienced so much grief and pain that we deserved this.

We flew to Jamaica in October of 2019. I expected a Rastafarian feel when I arrived in this small Caribbean island country, but what I experienced was exciting and different. The mountain peaks, the blue skies—it was an adventure, and it was sophisticated.

We married on a white-sand beach with Eric's best friends by our side, dedicating ourselves to one another.

Our honeymoon was an adventure in and of itself. We tubed down rivers, glided among the trees, and swam with the dolphins. I arrived home refreshed and ready to focus on my next goal.

I thought Neal would return to work after Phillip's passing, but he didn't. He stayed. And he challenged me.

"Neal, I'm so sorry. I just don't know how we got here. I didn't mean for any of this to happen."

It seemed like I sobbed to my son nightly. I begged for his forgiveness. My oldest son had died in a motorcycle accident, and I could not explain it. What had I done to make God so angry? He had been punishing me since I was seven. How could I make Him happy?

"Mom, stop blaming yourself. Sometimes life fucking sucks, but you didn't do anything wrong," Neal said. "It's how you choose to respond to what happens that matters. Phillip and Pop want us to be happy. We have to honor their memories and live every day for them."

His harsh words shocked me. I hadn't thought about fully living my life since my dad passed, and even less since losing Phillip. The thought of happiness terrified me. I believed that my circumstances needed to be perfect for me to be happy, and the thought of rebuilding a life of perfection virtually scared the shit out of me.

"That sounds great, but how?"

"Go out and see your friends. See the people who care about you. You're so full of fear that you refuse to do anything. You must stop being afraid."

I realized how right he was and that I had to restart my life. The thought of another failure made each of my goals seem insurmountable. I saw myself as helpless, hopeless, and anxious, and I began self-sabotaging.

THREE DAYS AFTER MY SON DIED, I'd received an email reminder that the *Girls on the Run* season would begin in a few short weeks. No. I was not in shape to encourage girls to reach their full potential. I couldn't make a difference in my own state of mind. I was still numb. I had to bow out. This time, I would do it with grace.

I sent an email to our site liaison and the Southeast Michigan Executive Director:

Ladies,

I received the email regarding Saturday's training. However, I will be unable to attend and hope someone will be able to attend in my place. I am in Florida coordinating transportation for my son who passed away only days ago. I'm still trying to figure out my participation in the season. I will be in touch as soon as possible.

Thank you,
Jodi

Within hours I received emails back telling me to focus on my current situation, take it a moment at a time, and that we would deal with the training later. These people I'd never met wished me their best, extended their condolences, and offered any support they could. I lay in my mom's bed feeling shocked. All the behaviors I wanted to repeat—the isolation, walking away from relationships—began to fall away. I was encouraged that people, even strangers, cared about my situation and well-being.

I followed their advice. I focused on my son, my needs, Phillip's memory, Neal, and my family. Finally, as people started to resume their daily lives, Neal encouraged me to begin a life as well.

I reached back out to our site liaison and explained that I still wanted to coach but couldn't guarantee my presence at each practice. My migraines had become uncontrollable again, and my grief was overwhelming. I wanted to rebuild a life, but I had to accept the reality of my health and live within those constraints.

Our site liaison asked to meet with me to conduct a short one-on-one training session to make up for the one I couldn't attend. We met at my co-coach's house in the evening. I knew God was calling me to change the way I responded to trauma.

Exhausted from a long day of grief, I showered, climbed into a pair of black leggings, then slid a sweatshirt over my head. I would never have worn this for an initial meeting with people before, but I had no energy to add makeup to my face to cover the grief. Teddy lay in the bathroom with me, his head cocked to the side, and he looked up at me. I knew he was curious about where I was going. I hadn't left the house in days except to walk him and Zeus, the Husky I'd acquired with Eric.

Looking down into his sad eyes, I said, "I have to go. My head is killing me, but if I continue to avoid people, I'll lose my mind. My sanity. My health. Neal will lose his mama."

I pulled up outside Jennifer's beautiful blue home, and she invited me into her modern farmhouse. We had an immediate connection. Her decor, styles, and our personalities were almost indistinguishable. Soon our site liaison arrived with the bag and shirt supplied by *Girls on the Run* and the season of supplies that we'd need, including a book of lessons for each meeting of the season.

Laura, our other co-coach who would also be attending our Monday and Thursday sessions, was there and was excited to discuss our lessons and how we'd put them into practice. I was grateful that she was a runner. I'd focus on the lessons, which highlighted social, emotional, and health skills, and she would lead the running. Jennifer would be present at our Thursday session to help with anything necessary. As a runner herself, she could help pace the girls and get them ready for the 5K they'd run at the end of the season in only twelve weeks. Laura and Jennifer were wonderful co-coaches, and I was thrilled to have someone there as a backup on days when I couldn't pull myself out of bed because the feelings were overwhelming or the migraines had become unbearable.

For the next twelve weeks, my goal was to attend two weekly training sessions. On the days I wanted to quit, these wonderful women encouraged me that I could do more, go further, and succeed, that I had it in me to show up for these fifteen girls in third through fifth grades.

I dug deep. I was determined to run this 5k with them. On the first day of the season, I learned that some of these girls were non-runners like me. They, too, had never run a 5k. I committed to running alongside them. I began walking. I jogged, then I walked when I got tired. But I never stopped. I was determined. I would do this for my son.

On days when the pain was too much, when my migraines were out of control, I would simply show up. I would cheer on my girls even if I couldn't participate.

The little eight-year-old girl who'd been lost since the automobile accident finally felt vindicated. She took part in each lesson and was encouraged to do her best. She was empowered and was taught to love herself. I continued to work on her in therapy. I continued to love and heal her.

I worked on healing each child within me, each little girl who'd been injured as a result of a trauma. I consoled them. I heard their voices, heard their pain, let them cry. Finally, I encouraged them to heal their wounds. The adult within me told them how strong they were, how they'd responded in the only way they knew how at the time. The love I'd been longing for began to grow from within me as I gave back to these girls and healed my emotional wounds.

The end of the season arrived too soon, and I was amazed when the girls showed up to run with their tulle skirts, their *Girls on the Run* shirts, and their enthusiasm. Each of us had learned something new about ourselves, something we'd take forward to help us on our journey.

The starting buzzer sounded, and we started. The girls in front of me ran, and I paced myself. I jogged, I slowed to a walk. I picked up the pace and jogged again. I encouraged the girls around me, my team, and other teams of girls who were present. There were hundreds of us—coaches, girls, and their parents—who had come out to give their support.

The ground around me was chalked with bright messages of encouragement in pink, purple, blue, and green: You can do this! You are wonderful! You are powerful! I soaked up this inspiration. There were signs, some held by supporters, others staked into the ground, that were messages of love to champion us to the finish line. I continued on. I didn't care if I finished at the end of the pack or somewhere in the middle. I was determined to finish what I'd started.

Finally, the finish line was in sight. I began to jog. I wanted to cross it running. And when I did, there were balloons and a hot cocoa bar waiting. Veterans handed me a medal. These veterans had come out to support me. I was overwhelmed.

I threw some marshmallows and sprinkles in a Styrofoam cup of hot cocoa and went to meet my team at the flag. We had a few runners left on the course, but overall, our girls were all here, jumping, running, and screaming about their success. My heart swelled with pride. I hugged each of them and waited for the rest of our team.

As each girl crossed the finish line and made her way to our team flag, I hugged her and sent her home with a parent. I told her I'd see her at our final party practice. Their faces shined with pride and matched my own.

When everyone had left, I retreated to my car, exhausted, ready to go home and clean up physically and emotionally. I leaned back against my headrest, my tears streaming freely. I had done it. This time, I'd chosen a different response to my trauma. Instead of separating myself from others, I drew them to me. Life wasn't a race; it was a journey. There would be times I would walk and times I would jog. I'd never arrive at a finish line. Trauma stays with you, but I had started the healing.

I surrounded myself with positivity to garner the courage to change my world. I took each tentative step with fear, but I kept going. It was time to find new goals that encouraged me to succeed. I would rebuild relationships. I would rebuild my career. I would help others. I would heal.

PART II

THE EFFECTS OF TRAUMATIC BRAIN INJURY (TBI)

13

WHAT IS TBI?

There are multiple definitions of a traumatic brain injury (TBI), but according to all sources, a traumatic brain injury—or an acquired brain injury—occurs when a sudden trauma causes damage to the brain. According to the National Institute of Neurological Disorders and Stroke (NINDS), a TBI:

> . . . can result when the head suddenly and violently hits an object, or when an object pierces the skull and enters brain tissue and disrupts the normal function of the brain. The symptoms of a TBI may be mild, moderate, or severe, depending on the extent of the damage to the brain and the period of time the person loses consciousness for. Other symptoms of a TBI include headache, confusion, light-headedness, dizziness, blurred vision, fatigue, changes in sleep patterns, mood and behavior changes, and difficulty with concentration

and attention. People who experience moderate or severe TBI's may show additional symptoms including headaches that get worse or do not go away, vomiting, repeated nausea, convulsions or seizures, slurred speech, numbness in extremities, a loss of coordination, and increased confusion, or restlessness or agitation.[1]

It's important to seek medical treatment for TBI as soon as possible since little can be done to reverse the initial brain damage caused by the trauma. Treatment is determined by a variety of factors, such as age and medical history. The extent and type of injury are also factors in determining treatment. Some people may only need rest, observation, and ice. Others may require sedation, assistance with breathing, or surgery. Determining appropriate treatment is complex because of the range in severity of traumatic brain injuries.

Once the initial treatment is complete, there are lifelong considerations to consider—and they're much different for pediatric patients than they are for adults. Ongoing treatment should also consider the transition to adulthood. If you are a parent reading this book, please ensure you make these considerations for your child.

I FIRST REALIZED THAT TBI had been applied to my medical records when I was living in North Carolina in 2008. I was seeing a neurologist and pain management physician for migraine treatment and seizure control. When I first saw

---

[1]   National Institute of Neurological Disorders and Stroke, "Traumatic Brain Injury: What Research Is Being Done?" https://www.ninds.nih.gov/health-information/disorders/traumatic-brain-injury.

the diagnosis on the MRI order, I was confused and believed there had been a mistake. I asked the neurologist about it at my next appointment.

She confirmed that, yes, I'd been living with a TBI for twenty-six years, ever since 1982 when the accident occurred.

"What's a traumatic brain injury? And why didn't they tell my parents about it in 1982?" I asked.

"You were diagnosed with an open head injury. A TBI is the result of an open head injury. They did tell your parents," she explained.

My face must have registered confusion; I know that my brain did. My eyes squinted, and my lips pursed at her statement. My parents had never mentioned the term *traumatic brain injury* to me.

Except for migraines and seizures, which I'd attributed to my head injury, I'd been relatively healthy, had good hearing and vision, had graduated from college summa cum laude, had maintained a marriage, friendships, and was a mother to two children. I couldn't see how this diagnosis applied to me. I thought traumatic brain injuries were reserved for veterans returning from war.

The neurologist's response had been casual, as if she explained this to patients daily, and I was just one of many. But the ease of her answer shook me. I thought that people with brain injuries had difficulty walking and talking and had trouble performing the tasks of daily life.

Sure, I occasionally struggled to find the right words, and growing up, I'd struggled with logic questions and math and processed things differently from my peers. And, yes, I still struggled with these things, but I'd overcome them, found a way to work around them. I hadn't had a choice. I'd always felt a need to explain myself to others when I struggled, but I didn't know why. Was this the reason? No—certainly, I didn't have a deficit. Wasn't that what a brain injury meant? Wasn't this a diagnosis reserved for people who couldn't live on their own?

Leaving the neurologist's office, I looked at the other patients in the waiting room. They all seemed like me, so normal. Did they have traumatic brain injuries too? I figured they were here for migraines or seizures. I knew neurologists saw patients for all sorts of reasons—Alzheimer's, brain tumors, Parkinson's Disease, strokes—anything having to do with the nervous system. But the people in this waiting room looked like they lived independent lives.

Could a person with a TBI lead an independent life without help from others? I thought about the things I did daily: I drove a vehicle, I took care of my children, I worked a full-time job. I had graduated high school and earned a bachelor's degree. I raised and took care of two children. Not only was I self-sufficient, but I cared for others. I cared for a whole classroom of children! If I was a TBI patient, were there other people like me who could do the things I could do, or was I an anomaly?

I needed to know more, and the first thing I did was call Sparrow Hospital to order my medical records from 1982. I knew it was a long time ago, and I held my breath in hopes that they still had my records. All my physicians had since retired, and the hospital was the only place I could hope to find answers.

"We do have records from that time, but it may take up to a month for us to get them to you. Do you want to wait for them?" The woman's kind voice offered me hope, but I wasn't sure how often they received this kind of request—a request for pediatric files over twenty years old.

"Yes, I want them. The x-rays, emergency room records, operative reports, everything," I answered, swallowing down the fear of what I might find.

"Okay. I'll email you the records request form. You'll need to sign and date it, and you can email it back to me. If you have any questions, please call me back." I knew their records department was busy and the lady was ready to get off the phone, but I heard a hint of curiosity in her voice.

About a month and a half later, I pulled the thick manila envelope of my pediatric medical records out of the mailbox. After the boys had gone to bed, I lifted the flap from the envelope and removed the photocopied pages. The lengthy printed materials were like a book in my hands. The chart held my medical history, laboratory and diagnostic reports, progress notes, physicians' consultations for each inpatient stay, all medication orders and operative reports, and the discharge summary for each inpatient stay. It seemed like there was no order to the record, although I'm sure there was. I took it apart and put things in chronological order, refusing to read until everything was organized by date.

I fell asleep that night, eager to read my chart the next day. On Saturday, I woke early and dug into my history. I read and reread the details, tears streaming down my face. I envisioned my small body on the emergency room gurney, then in the operating room. I'd had no idea about the details or extent of my injuries.

The doctors and paramedics who'd been involved in my care had become a part of my life after the accident, and each of them had told me they believed my survival was a miracle. I celebrated their careers and promotions with them, and eventually I attended their retirement parties. They always said I was their miracle. After learning about the severity of my injuries, I realized why they said that.

But why hadn't anyone told *me* exactly what happened? No one had ever said the words *brain injury* to me. They said I had a *head injury,* which sounded like it was nothing. My head was cracked open, they sewed me back together, set me on my feet, and sent me back to school. I'd made a full recovery. The whole thing had been glossed over, like I was a child who'd bumped my head on a dresser, had a couple of stitches, and recuperated.

The words *traumatic brain injury* sounded permanent, lifelong. It was vastly different from what I'd understood. I began researching what it meant to be diagnosed with a TBI, not just for my symptoms but for other people. Did their symptoms match my own? Did they also have migraines? Seizures? Had they struggled like me? Did their symptoms get worse over time?

I read article after article about TBIs, and I finally realized that our family had chosen to ignore my head injury. It had been easier and far less painful. It was easier than believing I had a wound to my brain, that my brain had been exposed to elements, and that it was a lifelong condition. An injury like this changes the brain's design—its function and operation—and they chose not to see that. After my wound was repaired, my hair grew back, and my injury became invisible.

And then I was expected to behave like the rest of my peers. My internal struggle was my own to deal with. I often felt frustrated and very, very alone. Although I attempted to communicate those feelings, I struggled with the shame of being different. When I was able to communicate my struggles, my voice was largely ignored. My pleas went unheard and unvalidated because I'd already proven that I could overcome the obstacles in my life.

This was a powerful realization for me as an adult. I no longer needed the validation of other people! I *had* persevered, and I'd done it on my own. I overcame many of these struggles. I'd survived.

Research

As I read my record and began researching TBI, I discovered that things had changed over the years. How they recorded brain injuries in 1982 was vastly different from what's done now.

In 1982, physicians classified head injuries as simply *open* or *closed*. An open head injury was when the skull was fractured or broken. A closed head injury was without a fracture. These classifications were relatively simple and straightforward. However, TBI research, advocacy, and certain organizations made growth and progress in the mid-1980s and 1990s. It wasn't until the Traumatic Brain Injury Act of 1996 Mandate was passed that it became a requirement for hospitals to create a uniform reporting system for traumatic brain injuries. Finally, public information regarding awareness, prevention, research, and assistance was funded by the federal government.

The federal government created a task force charged with determining the effects of TBI. TBI was one of the leading causes of death among children and adults in the United States, and in 1996, there were more than 5.3 million people living with TBIs. That statistic was staggering—5.3 million people just like me.

Over the next months, I read research articles about traumatic brain injuries and the progress regarding treatment: treatment for pediatric patients, treatment for adults who'd sustained injuries as children, and treatment for adults. I read blogs and stories from survivors, some like myself, who were looking for answers to medical issues they currently faced, unsure if they had anything to do with their injury. We all wanted to know how others were dealing with the ongoing symptoms of TBI and the effects it left on our lives.

My world had been shaken up. I now understood that some of the medical issues I faced were the result of a brain injury, and I felt overwhelmed by this new information. Coming to grips with the fact that my brain was somehow different from someone who had no injury made me feel like I was *less than*—again. Yet, reading about others and speaking with them inspired me. I saw the amazing things these survivors were capable of doing. They raised strong families and children, graduated at the top of their classes, worked jobs, and started businesses. The same things I was doing. Without extra support, we'd kept up with our peers in school, graduated high school, and met the same challenges as our non-brain-damaged peers. And because there hadn't been any research at the time, we'd done it on our own because we had no other choice.

The sadness and darkness, the shame I'd previously felt because of my brain injury, began to fade. I was transported from my black-and-white world of shame into a bright technicolor world. I was Dorothy. I had landed in Oz. In my blue gingham dress, I peered from my farmhouse door down the yellow brick road for the first time and realized that I, too, fit into this new world. And it was okay. There was no shame in fitting into this world where things looked slightly different.

As I read an article one evening, I let out a sigh, and tears welled in my eyes. I looked at a list of symptoms that children with a TBI experience. These were the exact comments I'd seen on my report cards: confusion, behavior changes, difficulty with concentration and attention. Next on the list was headaches. I remembered all the days I came home from school with a nagging headache. I thought about the days I'd sat beside the swings on the playground, too tired from a headache to play. And now I saw that other children had experienced these too. I wasn't alone.

And now, physicians and therapists were aware of these symptoms, and new solutions were being implemented in the schools for children with TBI. Children who faced an accident as I had, children who had traumatic brain injuries, would not have to struggle with the shame and pain I'd felt. Although my life hadn't been easy, I took comfort in the knowledge that my work had been done for another child, for other people. As much as I didn't want to fit in the category of TBI, it now felt good.

In the beginning, I looked closely at the pediatric symptoms and realized that I had many of them. Next, I looked at the lifelong symptoms of TBI and found that they, too, fit my situation. It became clear that this was not a day, week, or month diagnosis, but it required a lifetime of vigilant treatment.

The shame of my injury and struggles began to diminish. Phrases I'd heard while growing up like, "that was a long time ago," or "you should be better now," or "you can't blame it on your past," had bothered me for so long, and now I knew why. I would have to deal with a lifetime of effects. I felt vindicated that I no longer felt the need to justify myself for having a TBI. My injury wasn't simply a medical problem; it had caused my struggles with my memory, decision-making, social difficulties, and transitions in aging.

I poured through research about impairments in attention, memory, processing speed, and an inability to quickly switch my thinking about topics. Research showed that brain injuries affect a child's ability to self-monitor, self-regulate, plan, organize, and make decisions—details that influence a child's behavior and their interactions with other people, especially during their adolescent years.

I began to extend myself grace for the days I sat on the sidelines during recess and the months I cheered for peers in high school sports while longing to join in. Being separated wasn't my choice, but it was a developmental delay caused by a brain injury that wasn't my fault—a delay that caused irreversible damage that time couldn't make up, no matter how hard I worked.

Then I offered my family the same grace I was giving myself. I found detailed articles that reminded me of the trauma we'd survived as a family and how our lives had been so drastically changed in an instant. I found out that parents and caregivers feel challenged with a limited number of resources, a change in the family model, and their own depression. The data indicated that children from well-functioning families demonstrated better psychosocial recovery and that those effects were felt for years to come. I thought about my parents' well-meaning intentions. I had recovered for a sustained time. One bump in the road was not going to deter me from a lifetime of happiness. They'd worked hard to ensure that I had adequate support after the accident, and I wasn't going to let that hard work go to waste.

TBI AND DAILY LIFE

When I found an article titled "How TBI Affects Everyday Function" on the Northeastern University website, I felt a wave of hope. I compared the list with the ways I struggled and realized that many of them may be due to a TBI. The article mentions these typical difficulties for those with TBI:

- Concentrating on tasks
- Remembering new material
- Thinking, speaking, and solving problems slowly
- Reading for understanding quickly
- When normal routines are changed or when they are over-stimulated
- Moving on when encountering difficulties they cannot fix
- Finishing things within a reasonable timeframe

- Thinking outside the box, thinking abstractly, and using humor
- Finding words and/or understanding what others are saying when trying to communicate (oral and written)
- Taking turns in conversation
- Maintaining the topic of conversation
- Using an appropriate tone of voice
- Understanding and using sarcasm
- Responding to body language and facial expressions
- Keeping up with others in conversation

Yes, I sometimes struggled with concentration and solving logic problems. It was difficult to think abstractly, and I had a hard time maintaining a topic of conversation. I preferred jumping from topic to topic and sometimes couldn't find the right words. I didn't like to change my routine and found that I struggled when there was too much noise and light in a room. I was very easily overstimulated. When there was something that I couldn't fix, I couldn't move on because I had to focus on fixing it. Of course, some of the other items didn't fit me; I loved humor and reading. But it was clear that having a TBI had been life-altering, and it would be up to me to manage the effects.

I began keeping a daily planner. A paper planner. I wrote down upcoming appointments and detailed my days and the events that had happened. I referred to my calendar when I felt like I couldn't remember things.

I created lists—tons and tons of lists. I organized my life around to-do lists. I made an inventory list for our pantry and household goods, and I used it to create my grocery lists. I created lists of places we'd vacationed, inventory lists of my clothes and the kids' clothes, divided by seasons. I listed bills and their due dates. I created a list of meals and the ingredients required. I created lists for each of my physicians, listing each doctor, the dates and details of each procedure I'd had, and lists of the medications I'd been prescribed and the start and stop dates for each. I had lists of goals I was working on and books I was reading. Lists of logins and passwords, lists of gifts to give others, lists of projects I wanted to complete.

Then, one day, I lost one of my lists. I panicked. I searched the house. I ripped the cushions from the couch, took everything out of my car. I couldn't find it. I sat on the shower floor and sobbed. All the control I felt I'd gained over my life had been lost.

So, I searched for a better way.

I abandoned all the scraps of paper for an app I put on my phone and started again. This time, I could create folders for my lists, organize them by category, and determine if I needed them daily or if they could just stay there, hidden behind other lists until I needed to use them as a resource.

I'd found a better way to shore up my memory. I was taking back control of my life. I was determined to manage the effects of my TBI.

14

PHYSICAL AND EMOTIONAL ISOLATION

The cycle of isolation started the day of my accident, and it continues in a milder form today. What was meant to protect me eventually brought negative consequences.

For survivors of trauma—and TBI is a far-reaching trauma—isolation is a by-product and is caused by many factors. Initially, my parents isolated me. Doctors encouraged me to stay hospitalized, and then my parents encouraged me to stay home because of health concerns. I was out of school and disconnected from my peers for weeks. It was nice that they sent me messages of love and concern, but the world went on without me, and I knew it. I watched from my hospital room and then my home.

After I returned to school, I continued to isolate as a way to protect my emotions, a way to protect myself from feeling different from my peers. I could see that my friends continued to learn. They continued to work through their multiplication tables and spelling lists, but not me. I sat in a shocked state of mind, my brain solely focused on survival. When there were no imminent threats, my body and mind conserved their energy and stopped paying attention. In class, I was detached from my peers and the lessons. Anxious. Worried.

By the time I got home at the end of the day, I was exhausted. I felt like a ten-speed bike that had been shifting gears nonstop, not knowing which one I needed at what time. The chain was falling off my bicycle, but I was doing my best to keep the wheels going. So at home, I parked my worn-out-bicycle mind in my bedroom. I closed my eyes and rested, my brain overwhelmed and overworked. I recognized that I was processing things differently than I had before, and I was filled with shame. I felt stupid.

Kids can be mean, and my peers didn't let me forget how different I was. I was teased, excluded, bullied, and ganged up on. Naturally, the kids created new social circles based on common interests: sports, activities, shared classes, which neighborhoods they lived in, and even family connections. New cliques were formed, and I was left out, isolated.

Finally, in middle school, my peers pointed out my differences, such as the struggles I had with interpersonal relationships and my physical differences. I was filled with shame and embarrassment. Because I didn't know how to handle these emotions, I further isolated myself. My emotions were exhausting, physically and mentally. The need to escape the pain led to a further need to isolate. I withdrew to my bedroom.

As my headaches raged on as an adult, I isolated in pain more frequently. Later, when I filed for divorce, I again fell into these patterns of isolation. I was hurt and didn't have any other way to cope emotionally. So, I began to work through my PTSD from childhood.

Just as I began to heal, my father died. Unaware of any other coping mechanisms, I isolated from my family and friends for a year. It was the only way I knew how to survive the pain.

Three years later, when I lost Phillip, I knew I had to change how I responded to trauma. I could see my behaviors were destructive, but I had no other methods to rely on. I had to find a therapist I could trust and connect with, learn new coping strategies, and deal with this urge to isolate, so I could finally grow personally and emotionally.

"Dialectic Behavioral Therapy (DBT) teaches you how to live in the moment, deal with stress in a healthy way, regulate your emotions, and improve relationships." My therapist sat in the opposite chair and explained this new way of thinking to me. "Does this sound like something you'd be interested in trying?"

"I'll try anything. Seriously. You're the professional. Talking is not helping. I need to do something with all the shit I feel."

I'd been going to therapy for years, and I felt like nothing was working. I needed a change. I needed a solution, a way to take control of my life.

DBT provided me with a structured way to focus on myself. It allowed me to see how trauma had impacted my life, how trauma interfered with my ability to live. For me, it focused on the quality of my life. I set goals and began to plan a future. I began to see the situations that were in my control and the ones that were not. What was happening in other people's lives was outside my control, and I began to forgive myself for those situations. I started fighting for myself and working toward my future.

When things didn't go as planned, I felt less responsible. The need to isolate because I was ashamed of the results diminished. I hibernated in my bedroom for shorter periods of time. Although there were times when I became hyper-vigilant about my surroundings and the circumstances, they happened less often.

Through my work in DBT, I learned how to communicate my need for downtime to my friends and family. The time away from them was not meant to hurt them. I was not intentionally isolating from them; I was healing from the physical pain I felt. I gave myself permission to take time to heal my body. I taught my friends and family that the needs of my body were different from theirs and that my illness was invisible to them, but it didn't diminish my worth. I drafted auto-responses to emails for the days I was too sick to get out of bed. I left text messages unread and apologized when I needed to.

Isolating for medical reasons is still a very real part of my life. There's no cure for my migraines. There's no cure for a TBI. However, migraine treatment is improving, and there are new treatment options that have opened my world and allowed me to resume living. I've also found non-medical options that work for me. Lifestyle modifications such as consistent sleep and meal routines have become necessary parts of my life.

I have an app on my phone where I record details about my headaches, the dates they occur, their duration, the pain intensity, the medication or other relief methods I use, potential triggers, symptoms, and how the migraine impacted my daily life. This helps me communicate with my physicians about which medications are working, which are not, and what we need to change. I now play a key part in my medical care, bringing data to my physicians.

FINDING SOLUTIONS

Before I could change my isolation tendencies, I first had to recognize that it was a problem. What I discovered was that I isolated for both emotional *and* medical reasons. It's something I still struggle with today; the urge to isolate is ingrained in my personality. But I figured out what I needed to break the pattern. Here's what worked for me:

- I needed to find belonging.
- I had to let go of my past guilt and shame.
- I needed to give myself permission to have downtime to physically recuperate while still staying connected.

Trauma complicates lives. There's no getting around it. With TBI, it can complicate many areas of your life for years afterward. But I'd failed to realize that there were other people who understood how I felt, other people who felt the same way and had walked a similar path, and they could offer support. I really wasn't alone. But first, I had to open up and share what I was experiencing.

And I did that after Phillip died by sharing a post on Facebook. To my surprise, I received hundreds of responses to my first post. People related to my feelings and my words with an overwhelming kindness and support I'd never known.

From friends: "Jodi, my heart is hurting for you and your family. Surround yourself with love and support. Please know your sweet Phillip is with his grandpa now."

From previous colleagues: "Jodi, I am so sorry. I loved when Phillip came to my room to visit. His smile was contagious!" and "Oh Jodi, please feel our love and prayers helping you walk through this."

Mothers and fathers who had lost their children reached out to offer me support: "I am so incredibly sorry for this deep loss. It is truly a loss no mother should have to endure!! Sending you love and hugs for your endless ache and oxygen in the way of love when I know it is difficult to breathe! Love you more!!" and "Oh, I am so sorry. I know how you are feeling as I lost Shaun last year. If you need to talk, please contact me. I will keep the whole family in my thoughts and prayers."

The parents of Phillip's childhood friends reached out with loving arms and memories: "Phillip will be forever remembered and forever missed. We will cherish memories from our days with the boys at Midway Elementary, birthday parties, and Cub Scout camping trips. We are blessed to have known Phillip and will keep praying for strength for all of you in this unbearable time."

Over the course of the first year, I posted. On the most difficult days, on the days I missed my son, on the days I missed my father, on the days I was inspired by my guys, during the highs and the lows, I posted. Somehow, my posts created a message of love. And this love was reflected back to me.

Writing about my experiences and interacting with others on Facebook gave me a sense of community, a sense of belonging. Being in a group of grieving parents was awful, but knowing I wasn't alone made a difference. Other people had also lost their children through no fault of their own, and they experienced the same feelings of overwhelming grief and anxiety. And yet, they went forward every day. I felt empowered to do the same, empowered by each of their stories.

Instead of seeing myself as weak, I saw that such experiences occurred to even the strongest of people. For many years, I was taught that you attract your circumstances, you manifest your destiny. But I could not have attracted *this*. I could not have manifested *this*. I did not speak *this* atrocity into existence. It simply *was*. Shitty things happen to wonderful people—the wonderful people I knew and loved—and I needed to start loving myself and stop buying into what people who'd never experienced such pain had told me.

The new connections I made renewed my faith in friendships. If people weren't reaching out to me, then I had the courage to reach out to them. What had once frightened me now felt fresh and desired.

Since I no longer felt the need to isolate, I began to emotionally regulate my body, my relationships were less explosive, and the shame and embarrassment that had been a theme in my past began to fall away. Gradually, the windows of my mind started to clear. I began to see sunlight peek through shades. Finally, I built a door. I envisioned walking through it. Courage, I just needed courage.

My son, Neal, finally drew me through the door. Our late-night conversations, his wisdom, and sometimes, his brutal honesty drove me to analyze my life. I was determined to live again.

"MOM, THIS WAS NOT YOUR FAULT," Neal insisted.

The lights were too bright, and the tears just came. I was finishing the final touches to my makeup and hair, getting ready for our family Christmas. Eric and his sons were waiting in the living room. The car was packed. Again, I was on the ledge and didn't know how to get off.

Neal walked into our master bathroom, focused on helping me. I was glad he'd stayed for the year. He wanted to help me emotionally, and I wanted to help him through losing his brother. He insisted that I learn that I couldn't control every situation that involved the people I loved. All I could control was my response.

Neal talked me down. Focused me on the present. Talked to me about seeing our family. Finally, my breathing calmed, and I was steady enough to reapply my makeup and tug the hairbrush back through my tangled locks.

I controlled my responses. I controlled my emotions. I would not isolate. I would not isolate. People, my family and friends, would help me.

Not everything that happened to others was my fault.

Reframing Success

I unclipped the collar and leashes from Zeus and Teddy. My face broke into a grin as I listened to their paws skid across the cool tile to their water bowls. The heat from the afternoon was just what we needed. They needed a walk, and I needed space to think. We hadn't had *Girls on the Run* practice on Wednesday, and it was important for me to continue my walking schedule. It had only been a couple of months since Phillip's death, and I thought that if I just kept moving, I'd keep living. The pups were happy with the time outside, and I was happy to have their company.

My mind had wandered during my walk, and I'd fought the negative self-talk that crept in. I'd worked so hard to guard it from my mind, but the fear of not being able to run a 5k or finishing a race was present in my mind. I counted everything I had failed and longed to find success at something, anything, in my life.

I practiced the DBT skills I'd worked on and told myself that the strong, crushing feeling in my chest was only previous body memories, that I didn't have to listen to the negative self-talk. I only needed to be present in nature and watch what was happening around me. Count the birds. Count the leaves. Count my paces, my steps. Breathe.

My mind began to wander again. *Success looks different for everyone. Maybe you will finish the race, Jodi. You definitely won't be first, but you'll finish. I don't know if that is successful, but maybe with more work, you can be successful next year.* That self-doubt crept back in.

Count my paces. Count the leaves. Focus on the dogs' smiles. Walk, just walk. I stopped. Stunned, I realized that I was comparing myself to the measuring stick of *success*. I'd isolated because I felt unsuccessful! Did that mean I always had to be unsuccessful? I needed to really think this through, find out what success was, and if it was worth giving up on that pursuit.

When I got back home, I showered and changed, grabbed my laptop, and hit the Google search bar.

Define success, I typed.

According to Merriam-Webster Dictionary, "Success is the measure of succeeding, a favorable or desired outcome (also: the attainment of wealth, favor, or eminence); one that succeeds."

I already knew this. In fact, that didn't do me any good but made me feel worse. Attainment of wealth—ha! I didn't know any wealthy teacher or any teacher who was able to ask for eminence or favors. Shit, Google couldn't help me with this.

Wait. What about "one that succeeds"? Succeeds at what? Merriam didn't define this for me. Damn, this was not an easy task. Okay, go back, "a favorable outcome, one that succeeds." I needed to get serious and apply this to myself. Surely, I'd been successful at something.

I'd raised two kids. Okay, every parent did that. How do you measure it in terms of success? And I had lost one of them. Did that mean I was unsuccessful? Shit, don't go there, Jodi…

I finished college. Okay, yes, that was success. Damn, that was a long time ago. What am I doing now that is successful? Nothing?

I looked over at my dogs, that had now snuggled next to me on the couch. Teddy's eyes closed under the blanket, and Zeus rested his head on the arm of the couch. *Well, I'd succeeded in giving these two dogs a good life. I was a loving pet mama. This could be an example of success.*

I'd wanted a small dog so badly when I first got Teddy. I wanted to show him love and give him the best pet life ever. And this was a dream that had happened. When I met Zeus, I added to my pack and was doing the same for him.

I decided to take each small situation in my life and show myself that I could be successful, that I was successful. I would no longer measure my self-worth in dollars and cents or in corporate jobs, but in my current and growing capabilities.

My failure to recognize one goal didn't make me a failure. It didn't mean I had to withdraw in shame from the people I loved and feel defeated. It simply meant that I hadn't recognized a dream. From that day forward, my definition of success changed.

I began to reframe my experiences. Conversations that had begun with "Well, I used to be a teacher, but . . ." and "I worked in insurance, before . . ." changed to "I have a degree in elementary education and experience in the classroom," and "I have a master's degree in management and business, and business experience."

I reframed my experiences into positives, choosing to see my capabilities. Through deep conversations and soul searching, runs with the girls, and daily walks with the dogs, I envisioned new goals and set my focus on the future, knowing I could attain more.

Each positive experience, each success, no matter how small in the beginning, gave me courage. Each of these small building blocks I counted gave me the strength to speak about them with the friends and new acquaintances I met. This was in no way a long list of individuals! However, these people helped sustain me through the difficult first year after Phillip died. The image of a strong woman began to replace the weak, timid girl I saw when I looked in the mirror.

And that woman didn't want to be alone anymore.

15 **FRACTURED FAITH**

Before the car accident, faith, church, and God were a large part of my routine. We attended Catholic Mass on Sundays with my father. Mom carpooled me along with other neighborhood girls to catechism classes on Monday evenings. After the accident, we attended Sunday Mass with less frequency, opting instead to head over to Grandma's house early for breakfast and surround ourselves with family. I saw my father struggle with his faith. Why hadn't God interceded on my behalf? I began to question why God had allowed this to happen to me.

Eventually, my father would share the story, his feelings of desperation in the hospital chapel, begging God for my life. This is where his negotiations began. My father was a suit-and-tie businessman. Everything he did was for the benefit of our family. That day was no different. He simply went into survival mode the best way he knew how: fight or flight. He would approach it as a business deal, and he chose to fight with the power of negotiation, a weapon he knew well. He would negotiate with an invisible God whom he believed held my life in His hands. Dad's offer was to take care of me until his death. In return, God would give me life. My father knew he had no power over God, but he believed that he and God had reached an agreement that day. A miracle occurred, the miracle of my survival—all because of my father.

But there was an unintended consequence. Hearing the story about my father battling with God in the hospital chapel somehow diminished my value as a survivor. This was never my father's intention. He intended to give me faith in a higher power, but my child mind distorted that message. I interpreted that a higher power alone controlled my destiny, and when something negative occurred in my life, I felt like a helpless victim. I would question God. *Where are you? Why weren't you here to intervene on my behalf? Don't you care about me?* It took years of therapy to reframe that perspective and consider myself a survivor.

HOME AMONG THE FLOWERS and cards, I sat numb. I had no idea how I had gotten to this point. My father had died, and I was alone on the couch and confused. I had lost my faith in God. If he couldn't save my father, then what good was He?

I probed for answers in my morning journaling. I had to find out where this pain started. Why did I question His love for me? Why did I believe He did this *to* me? Why did I want to abandon this painful and dissatisfying relationship so desperately? To discover the answers, I wrote.

As a child, I was desperate to believe what my father had told me about negotiating with God for my life and his promise to take care of me in return. I'd wanted to know that my life was worthy of a miracle. And I believed this story, so I didn't feel abandoned by God—so that I could think that my father had some control of the situation.

However, as I grew up, I saw that God was not interceding in my life as He had when I was eight. The miracles were not accumulating as quickly as they had before. In my traumatized mind, God provided me with a single solution to my problem, yet it led to a series of new problems that I didn't know how to deal with, and I felt abandoned by Him. I couldn't understand why He would save me, only to let me fail.

I started negotiating with God in September of 1982. "Please, God, please just help me. I can't take any more bullying. I haven't done anything wrong since the accident. I will study more. I promise."

As my father's health waned, I believed that I could help him like he'd helped me. I could negotiate for his life. I would take care of him like he had taken care of me.

"God, if you please can help. Give the doctors clarity to help my father. Lord, I cannot lose him. I love him." Another negotiation failed. I felt like God was punishing me, but I didn't know where I had gone wrong or what I had done.

I didn't have a relationship with God yet, so I couldn't understand that He would provide me comfort, but He wouldn't grant me favors. My mind, in a hypervigilant trauma response, couldn't process this understanding. I was overwhelmed with the fear of losing my father. How could He have left at this point in my life when I needed Him so desperately?

And then the worst happened.

"God, what did I do?! You didn't even let me say goodbye to Phillip." I had no control. I wanted to die, to lie in the cemetery next to my son and father in the cold, packed snow, and die. I knew I couldn't because I had another son to live for, but that didn't change the deep emotions I felt, the desperation I longed for to have my child back in my arms.

I thought that I'd done something wrong, and God was punishing me for something I didn't even know I'd done. I tried to negotiate my way out of it, promise to do better, be better. I strove to be the best, do my best. It didn't change any situation in my life. I had no control over other people's survival. I only controlled my own.

Finally, I realized that I needed to forge my own relationship with God. I needed a personal relationship with Him. No one could intervene for me, and no one could speak to God on my behalf. When I forgave myself and forgave Him, it gave us permission to move forward in a loving and kind relationship. There was a purpose for the traumatic situations in my life. God had not abandoned me; He had walked beside me. Through my wounds, I had grown with Him in faith and emotionally.

IT WASN'T UNTIL SOMEONE REFERRED to me as a survivor that I considered what the word meant. I wondered if it applied to me. I'd lost my father, and it was 2018. I'd been diagnosed with PTSD, and I was in a constant state of threat, even when in a safe environment. My thoughts, my memories, the ones I couldn't control, played in my mind. I was doing my best to put one foot in front of the other, yet a friend of mine considered me a survivor.

This word did not seem to be applicable to me, and it felt odd in my mouth as I said to Eric, "Nicole said I'm a survivor."

I was not a wounded war hero. I hadn't survived an explosion, shooting, stabbing, or natural disaster. I was the victim of a drunk driver. And then I thought further. *A wounded warrior, a survivor of an explosion, shooting, or stabbing, the survivor of a major disaster—why couldn't I be the survivor of a drunk driver?* I could change my thinking. This wasn't something that had been done *to* me; it was just how the world was. And I could take credit for surviving it.

My thought process didn't change overnight. I started to see that God had walked with me through all my trauma and had given me the courage to keep going. I remembered that as a child, I'd prayed, "Thank you, God, for seeing me. Thank you for caring about me. Please walk with me and give me courage to go to school tomorrow. It is so hard, and I don't know how to do it. I wish you could save me." God didn't save me from my circumstances, but I drew on His experiences to guide me. I was a survivor.

I dug in deep and used my past as a building block to get through the loss of my father and the loss of Phillip. I continued to share, and friends and family continued to be compassionate, caring, and understanding in their responses. I turned to God. "Thank you, thank you for seeing me. Thank you for rebuilding my trust."

I had found relief. Where in the past I'd wanted to hide the truth about myself, it now felt good to talk about my past experiences. It felt good to talk about emotions I'd hidden for thirty-eight years. I was free to share my truth. Without judgment. Without shame. Because I was a survivor.

It had been my desire to live and my willpower to survive that caused me to take my next breath after the accident, the traumatic brain injury. God had not walked on this earth and pumped air into my lungs, but He'd provided medical assistance and given me courage and tenacity. *But I had done those things!*

It was time I used those character traits to take charge of my life again. I decided that if I controlled my survival, I would do the best I could to honor the loved ones I'd lost. And I would honor the people I loved who were still alive. I would take every advantage given to me and use it to the best of my ability. I chose to restart my life.

It took courage and time to realize that neither God nor my father saved me on September 2, 1982. I saved myself. I am a survivor. Yes, a miracle occurred that day. I do believe that it was a religious miracle; my faith testifies that it was through God. However, I had the will to live. There is no doubt about that. I dug deep from within and found the strength to fight for my life. I found the strength to return to the life I knew before the accident. I had no idea that it was not going to be the same, but I dug in, physically and emotionally, to survive.

Never let anyone else take credit for your survival.

16   **UNRESOLVED GRIEF**

As a girl, I got so sick of hearing "Get over it," and "Didn't your accident happen a long time ago?" or even "Well, you survived, right?"

Yes, the accident was a long time ago, and I survived, but I learned that survivors don't necessarily get over things. Our loss and our grief become ingrained in us. Like a lost limb or a scar, it's a body memory that's now a part of us. We learn to move on with day-to-day life, but we don't get over it. I couldn't change how others responded to my grief or the way I felt about my emotional angst and feelings, however strong or regulated they might be on any given day. That was hard for my family and friends because they wanted me to feel better and be who I was before, which was impossible.

Grieving is a process—a deeply personal process. Understanding and providing comfort to a grieving loved one is the most valuable part of that process. Furthermore, pushing a person to move on before they're ready stunts their growth. At least, that's what it did for me. As a child, I wasn't allowed to process my grief or the loss I felt about my childhood. I simply had to move on without feeling it. As an adult, I've been able to process emotions appropriately while grieving my father and my son. And oddly, through that grief, I was able to grieve my childhood. Although overwhelming, it has been extremely cathartic.

On the days the grief is less, it doesn't mean that I've forgotten about all that's happened. During some of my happiest moments, I talk about my father and my son. This, too, is how I process grief. Sometimes it's hard for the people around me to hear, but others find comfort in the stories I share. Either way, I learned that I don't have to be happy or sad but can choose to be both. I can continue to live, yet yearn for what I'd lost.

Grief is unlike a medical condition where you can eventually recover. There may be a set beginning to your grief, but there is no definitive ending. Some days the pain is dull, other days it's rough, and sometimes it's just as rough and jagged as the day my son and father died. The longer I carry the pain, the easier it becomes. The stronger I become.

DETACHMENT AS A FORM OF GRIEF

My symptoms of emotional detachment and PTSD began immediately after the automobile accident. This is not unusual for trauma survivors, but in 1982, I wasn't considered a trauma survivor. The child psychologists who saw me thought I'd recovered quickly, and I was released from intensive therapy only four weeks after the accident.

At the time, psychologists noted that during play therapy, I was preoccupied with automobile accidents and ambulances that took children to hospitals. They recorded patterns of anger that I expressed toward stuffed animals during our appointments. They described these behaviors as normal, given the circumstances, and explained that my anger and frustration would decrease over time.

However, I was embarrassed and frightened by my new and unusual behaviors. I didn't have the language to explain how or why I felt these new emotions. Instead, I began to hide the symptoms of my pain.

This created a situation in which I played various roles in each part of my life. I was a daughter, a student, a sister, a friend. I decided what the perfect image for each role should be, and I worked to imitate that. I watched other people and mirrored their actions. On the outside, I worked hard to become the girl everyone wanted me to be, but it was so hard. It seemed like everyone wanted something different, and I was being pulled in too many directions. Inside, I was a mess of emotions, vulnerable to suggestions, sensitive, depressed, angry, and anxious. I didn't know how to deal with the emotions of loss and grief, and I didn't know who I was or if I deserved any kind of future.

In the safety of my bedroom, I processed my rage. I hit stuffed animals, pounded on my floor and bed, screamed and cried, and confided each of these scary thoughts and emotions to Boo-Boo.

"**Ha, ha, ha! look at Grody cry!**" The middle school boys laughed at me yet again. I ran to the bathroom, angry and embarrassed. Lonely. This new middle school nickname had stuck, and my already-low self-esteem took another hit.

Walking to the sinks, I looked into the institutional mirror at my reflection. I did my best to wipe the tears from my face and calm myself. *Six hours,* I told myself. *Only six hours.* Another day of eighth grade. I could do it. I would survive, and high school would be easier.

The bell rang. Unnerved, I walked into first-hour English. I opened my notebook and began to write. I would share my feelings with Boo-Boo when I got home. I just had to hang on until the end of the day.

Throughout middle school, I continued to emotionally detach from myself and others. I had no one to turn to. Most days, I prayed that I would die because of the emotional highs and lows, the roller coaster of chaos I felt on a never-ending basis. In earlier years, I'd felt special because the doctors and my parents said I was a miracle. Now, the other kids called me *Grody* because of how I looked and the scars on my face. Their taunts devastated me. I felt alienated and disgusting, so I detached to protect myself. At that age, I couldn't know that this emotional detachment would affect my relationships in the future and create emotional instability when faced with future trauma. For now, detachment was a survival mechanism.

After my father died, I told my therapist about my distrust of the world around me and my fear of automobile accidents. I would pray for the safety and welfare of the individuals in the car and their families whenever I passed by an accident. Thirty-eight years later, my heart still raced, and tears sprung to my eyes. And I avoided public spaces with too many people because my throat closed up, and I felt like I couldn't breathe.

Being diagnosed with *complex* PTSD (CPTSD) meant I had more symptoms than those with traditional PTSD. I avoid situations that make me vulnerable and remind me of the traumatic events. I distrust certain people and the world in general, which causes difficulty in relationships. I'm often on edge, hyper-aroused, and jittery, and I may feel dizzy or nauseated when I'm reminded of the traumatic event. Because I've had multiple traumatic events in my life, I have more than the usual triggers or situations that leave me feeling this way.

I later found out that when the accident occurred in 1982, PTSD was an anxiety diagnosis reserved for children and adults with emotions and behaviors like my own. However, it was only applied to individuals who had pre-existing mental disorders, which I did not have, or to those who had suffered rape, assault, military combat, terrorism, bombing, torture, or natural disasters. I didn't meet the diagnostic criteria. Only five years later, the criteria changed, but it was too late for me to receive help. I had already slipped through the cracks.

Detaching from the negative emotions in my life became a problem from an early age. I was unable to identify my emotions or attach the corresponding emotions to what I felt. Eventually I would learn to break this pattern, but I had to start by recognizing the issue and when it occurred. I started by looking for patterns and the emotions that I refused to or avoided talking about.

Because I'd detached from my feelings, I couldn't share them with my husband or my friends. Instead, I used the same coping strategies I'd used as a child, and I played the role of what I envisioned was a perfect mother, friend, and wife. Some days, when the role became too heavy, I retreated. I avoided the people I cared about. Unfortunately, I lost many friends because of my inability to connect with the people I loved.

Being detached also meant that most of my relationships were one-sided. I had a great sense of admiration for the people I loved and cared about but couldn't understand why they cared about or loved me. I felt undeserving of their time and affection. I didn't understand why anyone would want to make me a priority in their lives. The stress and anger I felt about being unworthy and unable to communicate left me depressed. I no longer cared about the occasional fight or disagreement one has in healthy relationships. I agreed with people to keep them satisfied, unsure that they believed I was worthy of their love. This constant need for their approval left me feeling tense, angry, and resentful because I couldn't make other people aware of my true feelings. I simply went along with what other people said, did, what they thought I should do, and I acted in the way they thought best.

Finally, I hit a point of no return. I had lost interest in the future. The goals I'd been working toward died with my father in 2016, and the box stuffed with my anger, stress, and resentment exploded. I didn't know what I wanted from myself. Ever since my accident, I'd lived for other people. I felt emotionally damaged and thought that people with gaping wounds like my own couldn't achieve big dreams. In living for other people, I had died inside. I didn't know how to resuscitate myself. I thought about dying, and it seemed like a strong option.

Eric and my children supported me the best way they knew how through their love and constant companionship. I lived with Eric, and my sons constantly gave me the reassurance that life was indeed worth living for and that things would get better. I tried to hold on for them. I continued with talk therapy, but it wasn't effective. I needed real solutions to change how I saw myself and the world around me.

When Phillip died, I realized that I couldn't allow myself to live in the depressed, angry, frustrated state any longer. Living for Neal was my short-term goal, and until I could get better and live for myself, I would give him the best version possible of me. I decided to work toward getting better. I was determined to process my dark emotions, let go of my grief, and find the love I'd once felt. It had been there. It was a distant memory, and I dug deep within to find it again.

As a grieving mother, there was no role for me to fill, no one else's behaviors to imitate. I was simply on my own. The emotions were raw and overwhelming. I didn't know what to do with them. When I released my emotions on Facebook, I hadn't known the reception I would receive would be so kind and caring. My posts continued, and I began talking about them in therapy.

There was no beauty in processing these emotions. I wish I could tell you that it was easy, and I simply sat in a room, looked at pictures of people's faces and emotions to determine how I felt, identified the emotion, felt it, and processed how I felt about it. But that wouldn't be fair to you, and it wouldn't be an accurate portrayal of the difficult and often ugly work necessary to restore my sometimes-childlike heart.

My old scars were peeled open again. I cried out in emotional pain, shut down before I was willing to open up again. I often refused to admit to myself or anyone else the depth of the pain I felt. I knew I had to get to the root of my self-hatred if I wanted to heal.

I learned to change the way I processed emotions to new problem-solution skill sets. By improving my skills, my relationships and my confidence in them improved. I felt less need to isolate and was able to open up more with my friends.

However, the hypervigilance I experienced as a result of the CPTSD was still very real. I saw the world as a dangerous place after the death of my father. I knew this had to change when Phillip passed away. DBT therapy helped me to improve.

My new problem-solving skills learned from DBT allowed me to slow down and see solutions through a new lens and a new perspective. The world seemed less dangerous. I became less embarrassed about myself and began to open up to friends and family about my past experiences. The grace that was extended to me was overwhelming.

Previously reluctant to take on new tasks, I began to stretch myself in new ways. Kitchen skills and spatial and logic problems do not come easily for me, and I continue to work on them. Although I may struggle, I explain to the people around me the difficulty I have and that I don't need help, but I'm happy to try to complete the skill on my own.

This has been a difficult change for the people who love and care about me. They used to swoop in and rescue me, afraid to let me struggle. But now I'm no longer ashamed of my struggles or difficulties. I know that I cannot do everything perfectly, and I no longer hold myself to impossible standards.

The interpersonal relationship skills I learned in DBT helped me gain confidence in explaining my situation without embarrassment. My explosive emotional responses diminished, which led to improved relationships. These new, regulated emotions became a new pattern as I began to process my overwhelming emotions.

The final area I learned about in therapy was body memories. Your brain isn't the only place memories are stored. Memories are stored in our bodies at the cellular level. Think about it: remember a special birthday, being surrounded by loved ones, a cake is set down in front of you. Each of the people you love shares a smile with you, and they begin to sing the happy birthday song. These special traditions— memories—send warmth to your heart, your stomach, and wrap you in a sensation of love and family. I have these body memories too.

I also have negative body memories, which means that my trauma is stored in my cells as well. These body memories are a way of processing and telling the story of my trauma. Sometimes for trauma survivors, there's a long process before body memories come to the surface. Even when you distance yourself from the trauma, the body remembers it on a physical level.

Processing these body sensations for me meant feeling the automobile accident as if it were happening all over again. I experienced headaches, shaking, jerking, and trembling.

These experiences were usually triggered by stress. This left me exhausted and drained, but it has been an important part of my healing. After my father died, I released an extensive amount of body trauma, and then again after Phillip passed away. Now, I release body trauma with less frequency, but I know that it's still deep within me, and I know when it's present and triggered. Being open and aware of my body memories has been essential in my recovery.

17

CHALLENGED RELATIONSHIPS

After my accident, my parents provided me with a safe and nurturing home; however, they were unable to help me navigate school and friendships. My uneasy feelings created emotional dysregulation and strained relationships, and these instabilities factored into how my identity was formed as a child. I was either very closed off or extremely open with the people I surrounded myself with.

When I returned to school in third grade, I was still very detached, and I watched as my classmates met new developmental milestones. They picked out new library books that required a longer attention span and more detailed vocabulary. I continued to mull around with the younger kids, frustrated and falling behind. I faced difficulties outside of school that my peers couldn't imagine and had acquired a new understanding of medical terminology, yet I found reading Nancy Drew books a challenge.

I didn't have the attention span to finish a chapter. The other girls exchanged books each week, but I rechecked out the same book week after week, determined to finish. I avoided their looks. Mrs. Diamond attempted to guide me toward the books I'd read in second grade, but I wasn't deterred. If Nancy Drew was what my friends were reading, then that's what I'd read too—even though my brain couldn't comprehend the text on the pages.

"CINDERELLA, DRESSED IN YELLOW, went upstairs to kiss a fellow," the girls sang in unison.

Tears in my eyes, I stood next to Mrs. Diamond on the third-grade playground. Her hand was a comfort on my shoulder as I watched, frustrated, in the warm May sun. The two long jump ropes turned in opposite directions, and the girls jumped simultaneously. "Made a mistake and kissed a snake. How many doctors did it take?"

Double Dutch. I'd learned to jump double Dutch in second grade, but now I stood there, helmet lopsided on my head, unable to participate. The girls continued to jump, "1 . . . 2 . . . 3 . . . 4 . . ." Standing outside this important growing social circle was another way I was segregated from my friends.

My difficulty fitting in with my peers began in third grade, but it didn't end there. It was only the beginning. The little voice inside of my head that chanted *I'm not good enough . . . I'm not smart enough . . . I can't do anything right* became louder every day. I didn't know how to make it stop, and eventually it became so loud that I avoided relationships altogether. Already self-conscious about what my peers were saying, this little voice inside my head diminished my self-worth, my ability to focus, and my ability to respond to a range of emotions. The voice had become toxic.

That voice turned into a shout during middle school as I realized *I'm not pretty . . . I have bad luck . . . nobody likes me . . . no one will ever love me . . . everything is my fault . . . why am I even alive?*

In high school, the voice changed to *I don't want to do my homework . . . I don't want a curfew . . . I suck at math . . . she doesn't like me . . .*

The little voice was crying out in fear, crying out because I didn't want anyone to give up on me, even though I'd given up on myself.

Each time I created new attachments and relationships as an adult, that little voice returned. Since I'd had few opportunities to form healthy childhood relationships, I became avoidant and ambivalent about friendships. When faced with inconsistent friendships, I looked for clues about how my behavior influenced the outcome, how what I'd done affected the negative responses of another individual. I felt like I was on a teeter-totter of emotions. I wanted what I couldn't have.

At school, I faced avoidant and insensitive responses from friends. These friends were no longer emotionally available to me, which caused me to avoid relationships. I always felt abandoned and attempted to be self-reliant at school, yet I felt isolated.

I carried these emotional patterns into adulthood, forming relationships with the same patterns of behavior, looking for my mistakes that drove people away, then becoming emotionally unavailable, so I wouldn't be hurt. I minimized the importance of the loving and healthy relationships I did have. I couldn't understand why people would want to have a relationship with me. I believed that my family was only with me out of obligation rather than a sense of love. I couldn't understand the emotional depth that came easy for others and didn't understand the compassion and love that existed in healthy relationships.

In retrospect, when we moved to North Carolina, my ambivalence toward friendships became glaringly clear. I had the opportunity to meet a variety of new people, but I was emotionally unavailable. I was scared by the trauma of my past. I was depressed and withdrawn. I stretched to make friends but considered myself socially awkward, so I reverted to my middle school responses and patterns. I relived those same emotions again.

After I returned to Michigan and was divorced from Rich, I was determined that, through therapy, I would let go of these emotions. I became aware of my patterns and self-talk. I stopped telling myself that people didn't want to be with me and started attending social events. I enjoyed going to baseball games, football games, art festivals, etc.

But when my father died, all that stopped. I withdrew, repeating the mistakes and patterns of the past. The negative self-talk told me I was worthless and that relationships with me were not worth having. I longed for personal contact but couldn't tolerate it. Then when Phillip died, I knew that I needed to change my behavior. I focused on changing my self-talk to improve my confidence and improve my relationships.

Part of the reason for my *complex* PTSD diagnosis was the guilt and shame I carried. Complex PTSD is often described as the *relationship* part of a trauma disorder because it affects how an individual interacts with others. Guilt and shame are essentially social functioning emotions.

The automobile accident caused me an immense amount of shame. I felt a great sense of responsibility because my family members had come to East Lansing to pick me up. Mom and Dad had reassured me that the accident was not my fault; however, it did little to absolve the shame and guilt I felt.

Blaming myself for the death of my grandmother and for the critical injuries to others was complicated, and the story I often told myself was convoluted and problematic. While I knew about the actual events, I would often confuse them and place the blame on myself. The weight of this responsibility took a toll on my emotional and physical well-being.

"GOD, WHY DID YOU MAKE ME DO IT? Why did you make me say yes? I could have said I didn't want to go to Aunt Ginny's house. Then none of this would have happened, and we would all be okay. No one would be mad at me!" I screamed into my pillow night after night, tears flowing, my trusted Boo-Boo by my side.

Although I blamed God, I felt responsible for the accident, responsible for the pain and struggle my family dealt with. The accident was caused by a woman I didn't know, a person who was faceless and nameless to me. Because I didn't see anyone take responsibility, I did. The pattern of taking responsibility for situations that I didn't cause would span into my adulthood.

Lifting my head, I looked at Boo-Boo. "You're my only friend now. No one wants to be friends with a scar-faced girl. I'm bald and ugly. I'm horrible. Like a monster. That's what I could be for Halloween. No one wants to see me or look at me. I'm ugly and stupid. I can't do multiplication, and I can't remember anything at school. I hate myself!" I was crippled with shame.

Occasionally, friends would still reach out to me; however, I was afraid to interact with my peers. I often declined invitations to go to a friend's house because I'd become anxious about the situations I had created in my mind. When I did accept invitations, I arrived hyper-aroused, anxious, and had already tormented myself into believing they didn't really want me there. I thought their parents had forced them to include me.

The summer between sixth and seventh grades, my aunt and uncle invited me to stay with them in California for a few weeks. This meant I'd stay with cousins who would teach me all the cool stuff every seventh-grade girl wants to know. With a little freedom, I learned a lot about myself. I learned about curling my hair, putting on makeup, and what it meant to be a cool teen, but most importantly, I learned a lot about positive self-talk. I listened to how my cousins talked to themselves and to each other, and when I returned home, I was determined to model that behavior.

UGH! HE NEVER HELPS ME WITH ANYTHING! I have to do the laundry, do the dishes, get the kids to soccer, feed the dog, make sure the lawn is taken care of, and remind him to take out the trash. He can't even put his cup in the dishwasher! I just want to throw the mug against the wall. I knew I was blowing it out of proportion. Rich hadn't helped with the dishes. It really shouldn't have been a big deal, but I was so angry.

Jodi, it's your fault. You are not enough. All moms do this. Why are you complaining? You have a roof over your head, two beautiful boys, a wonderful mom and dad, a great brother, a nephew, and a sister-in-law who you adore. You should be able to do it and more. You don't have the energy. You have headaches. You can't control them. You don't know how. You're lazy. You should just do it. Lazy, lazy, lazy. It shouldn't have been a big deal; I knew that. My inner voice turned the frustration I felt into guilt and shame.

I picked up the mug, put it in the dishwasher, sat down on the floor, and cried. *Why aren't I enough? Why can't I be good enough? Why can't I be like my friends? They have the strength to do this. They have the energy to take care of their house and enjoy time with their kids and husbands. But I'm exhausted. My brain and body hurt. I'm not worth the breath I take.*

This was the kind of self-talk I'd repeated to myself before my sons and I moved back to Michigan. Eventually, through DBT and other therapies, I was able to curtail it, but I reverted to destructive practice when both my father and son died. And each time this inner critic filled my head, I knew that I was inferior and weak.

Changing my inner dialogue wasn't easy, but like I'd learned from my cousins in seventh grade, whenever I became aware of it, I made a conscious effort to turn it around.

I noticed that I said things to myself that I'd never say to a friend or my child. Then, I saw that I said these things to myself when I was struggling with something or was frustrated. Those were the times that I could learn to treat myself better.

Soon I was calling myself out when I said things that weren't true. For example, I'd tell myself that someone else did something better than I did. But I didn't have any evidence to back up that statement, so I started to improve this part of my thought life.

When I started paying attention, I heard my complaints about how much I hated things. I hated doing the dishes. I hated bad drivers. I hated missing phone calls. I hated returning calls. I hated politics. I realized that I didn't actually hate these things at all. I love talking to friends and family on the phone, so returning their phone calls was wonderful. But returning business phone calls was just okay. I could be neutral. I didn't have to affix an emotion to everything. I could dislike doing the dishes. I could be frustrated with bad drivers. Missing phone calls could be an irritation. I was in control of how I chose to describe my situations. I thought, *My inner critic needs a larger vocabulary.* I swapped the word hate for something that better fit the situation.

When my inner dialogue became excessively destructive, I started talking to myself like a friend would. A friend would never tell me that I'm stupid or to shut up. Whenever my critic became destructive, I knew that I'd isolated from others for too long and that I needed some connections and—more often than not—a good laugh and a glass of wine.

When I finally got a handle on my self-talk, I decided to improve my relationships and communication skills. It wasn't easy to admit that I'd caused some of the issues in my relationships. It was easier to blame other people than take a critical look at myself, and that's what I'd been doing my entire life—blaming others.

During my therapy sessions, we focused on interpersonal relationship goals. My first goal was to keep my self-respect and communicate effectively. This had always been a challenge for me. Whenever I felt like I was losing self-respect, I began to communicate in negative terms. The little voice inside of my head repeated *I'm not good enough. They think I'm stupid.*

Whenever I felt disrespected or neglected, my communication would become aggressive, and that needed to change. I learned to communicate my needs effectively without being overly critical and mean. Fast-forward to my new marriage, and I practiced with Eric.

"Eric, I ran errands all day and went to practice, and I'm tired."

My sons were grown, but Eric's boys lived with us, and I wanted them to do the dishes that night. I thought one of them could load the dishwasher, and the other could empty it when it was clean. "It would be really nice if they could help me today," I said.

In that situation, I used my DBT skills and employed the **DEAR** technique:

Describe the situation: I'm tired and need help.
Express: I'm tired and need help.
Assert: They need to load and unload the dishwasher.
Reinforce: Reinforce my gratitude.

When I thought about employing this approach, I found I was no longer complaining, "I'm tired. Why can't someone else help? I do everything." The truth was that I *didn't* do everything. But I would get so caught up in my emotions that I would zoom in on the negative, and the little voice would scream, *Nothing is fair!* and *I can't!*

I didn't get it right every time. Not even close, but I'd started to change the way I thought, so I could change the way I communicated, so I could improve my relationships.

I also liked the **GIVE** acronym:

Be **G**enuine
Maintain **I**nterest
Validate
Have an **E**asy Manner

By being genuine, I could express my true self without trying to change anything to fit in.

When I showed interest in someone else, the relationship could become reciprocal, where we both contributed and received. I could show interest by maintaining eye contact and staying focused on the conversation rather than looking away or glancing at my phone. I validated the relationship by listening without judgment and acknowledging what I heard rather than pushing my agenda. And having an easy manner meant that I could smile, use humor, and be easygoing in my communications.

The **FAST** approach was also helpful:

Be **F**air
No **A**pologies
Stick to Values
Be **T**ruthful

To be fair, I had to be fair to myself, as well as the other person. No apologies meant that I had to stop apologizing for everything: for making a request, for breathing, for taking up space, for being alive. I also had to stop apologizing for having an opinion or for disagreeing with others. Sticking to my values meant that I would no longer abandon what was important to me to please someone else, and being truthful meant that I wouldn't lie, exaggerate, make excuses, act helpless, or depend on someone else when I could take care of myself.

Whew! What a tall order! When I started doing these things, other people started respecting me, and I started respecting myself. And I could finally form mature, adult relationships. The final part of DBT that helped me improve my relationships was *radical acceptance*. For me, this was life-changing, and it wasn't easy. It was so much easier to live in a state of anger and bitterness. Radical acceptance meant I had to completely and totally accept that I couldn't change the facts, especially the ones I didn't like. I had to accept everything in my life with my entire self: my mind, my body, and my spirit. Because I hadn't accepted the pain of my past, I'd gotten stuck in unhappiness, bitterness, anger, and sadness, and as a result, I'd created my own suffering.

I knew I had to look at my father's death. I'd been angry and resentful that I couldn't save him, and I took this anger out on the people around me. The first step was to identify the cause of the event, and I identified the facts without judgment or blame: *My father died, and I couldn't save him.* I looked at that fact without judgment. Yes, that fact had caused me pain, and I now had to free myself from that pain.

Step two was where things got rough. I had to explore and accept the feelings that went with my feelings about not being able to save my father. I wanted to shut down. Everything in me told me to shut down and stay safe, but DBT taught me that if I faced this, my life would get better. So, I trusted the process.

I created a list of feelings: anger, fear, resentment, frustration, sadness, shame, guilt. I located each place in my body where I felt these feelings, each sensation I felt. The anger rose in my stomach, bile in my throat, and a throbbing in the base of my skull and neck. The resentment caused a racing heart rate, furrowed brow, and scowl. I fully felt each emotion, however painful. The tears came, and I reminded myself that I couldn't change what happened, but I could release the physical pain that accompanied these emotions. Sometimes I had to sit and allow the emotions to wash over me. It was difficult but, in the end, a purifying experience. The tears rinsed away years of pain, which I'd stored in my body.

Finally, I had to be proactive about coming to terms with what had happened and improve my current situation. I used my mindfulness exercises to make decisions about what to do next. I wanted to trust that the people I loved were safe. I wanted to feel less anxious about losing them. I wanted to know that it wasn't my responsibility to keep them safe or save them. I needed to be realistic.

None of these new behaviors or thoughts were immediate for me. I worked at them until I believed in them. And after a while, I began breaking patterns. I began to see other events in my life that had caused me pain that I needed to reconcile and accept to move forward. I began creating lists of things I needed to accept and worked the process on each of them. By creating my new reality, I was creating new solutions and a new life.

I was encouraged as I began solving my own problems. I saw my health improve, and my relationships got better. Situations that I thought would never get better started to ease, and my anxiety was falling away. DBT taught me how to manage my emotions and improve relationships, and that, in turn, gave me a new life—a new life where I went from a survivor to a thriver.

EPILOGUE

Having a TBI has changed me. I can't say if it's made my life more difficult or not since I'll never know the difference. Occasionally, I find myself falling back into old patterns of thinking that life would have been easier if my brain injury hadn't ever happened, but I've learned how to turn my thoughts around. I use my DBT techniques on a regular basis. I still grieve the loss of my father and my son, but I wake up each morning with a smile on my face and hope in my heart. I remember to celebrate their lives instead of living mine in desperation.

Although my husband, Eric, played an important part in my journey, we decided to part ways. Nothing about divorce is easy, and I've learned to be open about my feelings and accept responsibility for my contributions. I'm proud that I had the strength to realize that I was in another unbalanced relationship where I gave more than I was capable of. I'm stronger now, and I have the skills and the drive to pursue my best life. If I'm lucky, I'm only halfway through this life, and I believe the best is yet to come!

Living with a TBI requires daily discipline. I'm limited in some areas, but I'm unlimited in my capacity to give and receive love, to have a fulfilling life, and to make a positive impact on the world.

And so are you.

ACKNOWLEDGMENTS

Nancy Erickson, The Book Professor*, my publisher, writing coach, and friend—I am eternally grateful for your dedication and the endless hours of help and support you provided to bring my story to life. You gave me the vehicle to tell a story I've longed to tell for a lifetime. You encouraged me to see my strength and gave me the courage to continue writing.

I could not have written this book without the support of my writing cohort, who provided me with authentic feedback: Nicole, Marybeth, Gisele, and Bruce. Your words were kind, caring, and without judgment. Thank you for your support and love as we walked this emotional journey.

ABOUT THE AUTHOR

J odi Gilroy always said that publishing a book was on her bucket list, and as a writer, educator, and trauma advocate, she was determined to make it happen. Even in chaos, she found peace in writing. Her book, often written through the lens of her inner child, healed her and will hopefully inspire you to begin your healing journey as well.

Jodi is a Strategy, Leadership, and Change Management consultant with a background in elementary education. She enjoys the beauty of living in mid-Michigan, her son, her dog, and all that is uniquely curious and whimsical.